ITALIAN FOR EDUCATED GUESSERS

Shortcuts to the Language

C. Peter Rosenbaum, M.D.

ITALIAN FOR EDUCATED GUESSERS: Shortcuts to the Language
Published by Forza Press

ISBN 0-9614045-1-5

Address all correspondence, both editorial and commercial,
to Forza Press, 521 Entrada Way, Menlo Park, California
94025.

Printed in the United States of America.

CONTENTS

PREFACE

THIS BOOK IS . . .

This book is for students of Italian who, like me, enjoy the language, want to be able to use it, do not have one of those disgustingly talented ears that seem to absorb everything on first hearing, but do hate the drudgery of rote memorization.

This book is for people who have completed the equivalent of one term of college Italian, who have grappled with it sufficiently to be ready to see patterns in what was originally entirely foreign.

This book is not intended to supplant traditional texts and grammars; those are necessary if you are to learn the basic structure of the language. This book, however, will make acquisition of certain important aspects of the language much, much easier.

This book will be particularly useful for people who will be spending time in Italy. Much of the material was suggested by spoken and written Italian I encountered during three years spent in Italy.

HOW TO USE THIS BOOK

You will probably be ready to start using this book after you have had the equivalent of one term of college Italian. Each chapter starts with introductory remarks. The chapters are placed roughly in increasing order of complexity or difficulty of the material, and many of them presuppose that you have mastered the material of earlier chapters. Many of the shorter chapters have been placed between the longer chapters to lighten the pace of the book.

Look over the chapter beginnings to see which ones might be for you now, which ones to defer. If your class hasn't studied verbs irregular in the present yet, the presentation of them here could be confusing to you. But once you <u>have</u> studied them, the material here might well boost your comprehension of them with only a modest additional effort. Again, this book is intended to complement the text you are studying.

ABOUT THIS BOOK

As my comprehension of the language grew, a number of patterns, rules, and ways of learning the language appeared to me. For the most part, these were never stated in the numerous textbooks and grammars I had studied. These shortcuts often allowed me to make a correct Educated Guess about a word or phrase I had never seen before.

These shortcuts are passed along to you here in much the same manner as they came to me. A series of words or phrases is presented, and you are often invited to discover the common pattern in them for yourself, before seeing the pattern stated in the text. Quizzes abound, to let you test your ability to make Educated Guesses in situations where you previously thought yourself to be totally ignorant. See Chapter 6, "Faking Out Irregular Past Participles," for an example.

Parts of the book require rote memorization; after all, a certain amount of it is unavoidable. The material that must be memorized is important. For example, the words and phrases found in Chapter 7, "Popular Italian Words and Phrases," are very commonly used ones.

Still other parts of the book are reference sections, where you can look for things when you need them. The expressions are presented in context, to make it easier to use them. Chapter 14, "Yesterday, Today, and Tomorrow: Expressions of Time," provides an example of this feature.

Finally, interspersed throughout the book, there is material that was written simply because I found it interesting and hope that you will, too.

This book has been incubating for over two decades, as a labor of love with the Italian language. It is both serious and affectionate. I hope that, as you read it, you will not only learn but also have fun.

ACKNOWLEDGMENTS

Teachers and Support

Paolo Candela taught an excellent Italian class at Georgetown University during 1958-59. At the University of Genova, during 1968-69, Maria Gianelli was a gracious and patient tutor, and Romolo Rossi and Giandomenico Sacco assisted with many translations, written and verbal, that made that my year of transition from superficial knowledge to deep immersion in the language. During 1975-76 at the Stanford-in-Italy campus in Florence, Franca Celli and Joan Mammarella McConnell shared their superb understandings of English and Italian with a number of grateful students, of whom I was one. In the summer of 1981 our class in Italian grammar learned much from Prof. G. R. Orvieto of the **Università Italiana per Stranieri** in Perugia. In 1982, Franca Pezzoni of Genova reviewed numerous lecture drafts, providing much valuable learning of grammar and idiom.

The Fulbright-Hays Commission supported sabbatical years in Genova during the 1968 and 1982 academic years. Cipriana Scelba and Gladys Semeryan were among those who were most helpful in allowing those exchanges. Stanford University made it possible for me to teach in Florence during the 1975 and 1982 academic years.

Reviewers

The manuscript has had the benefit of review and critique at many junctures. The earliest reviews were by Romolo Rossi and Vicenzo Traversa.

Josephine Guttadauro prepared all the middle drafts of the manuscript. Her feel for English and Italian, and the many helpful suggestions made by her family, provided valuable contributions -- in addition to her impeccable typing.

Several students at the Casa Italiana at Stanford (Palo Alto branch) were meticulous in the reviews and comments on middle drafts, especially Susan Cromwell, Virginia Francis, Christopher Pryor, and Sally Martin.

Contributors

Nearly 30 years of friendship with Gennaro Fusco have been richly rewarding, and one dividend of that friendship has been an introduction to many words and expressions that appear in this book.

Under the guidance of Joan Mammarella McConnell and Maria Grazia Passini, a number of students at Stanford-in-Florence made many useful suggestions of current English and Italian expressions and of Faithful and Quasi-Cognates.

Virtually all the material in Section II of the chapter "The Subjunctive (with Flowcharts)" came from materials presented and discussed in class during 1975-76 by Joan Mammarella McConnell.

David Hood, Orlando Lucero, Bernadette Luciano, Katherine Luciano, and Massimo Prati reviewed and made substantial contributions to several chapters.

In 1982, Franca Celli did a meticulous review, ferreting out errors of fact and nuance and supplying many valuable suggestions for ways out of etymological thickets.

Francesco Marincola gave the book a final **controllo** and provided a number of useful additions and examples.

Ralph Mapson did the drawings.

Arnold Abrams of REPROGRAPHEX provided useful advice and encouragment at many junctures and supervised the production of the camera-ready copy.

Ron Lewton edited the manuscript and helped design the book. His unerring eye and editorial judgment were invaluable, as were his diligence and care.

For any errors that have persisted into publication, I take responsibility.

C. Peter Rosenbaum
Menlo Park, California
November 1984

ONE

HOW TO BE
AN EDUCATED
GUESSER

PATTERN RECOGNITION

What Pattern Recognition Is

Many parts of this book involve pattern recognition. Soon there will be brief quizzes to help you use the book well. By pattern recognition we mean an ability to see similarities and parallels where none had been pointed out to you before. Once having seen the similarity or parallel, you can then develop a rule or principle that will allow you to guess at or predict other words or phrases that follow the same rule. In short, you can see a pattern and make an Educated Guess as to other words that fit the same pattern.

You should be able to use the idea of Educated Guessing at many points throughout the book and find that you know a lot more Italian, or can learn it with much less effort, than you may have thought!

Three Miniquizzes and Answers

Please take the three miniquizzes that follow before looking up the answers for any of them (this to prevent inadvertent peeking). Answers start on page 3.

1

Miniquiz 1.   You will be presented below with a list of five pairs of English words and their Italian counterparts.   Then you will be given two more English words, but not the Italian, and you are to make an Educated Guess as to what to enter in the blanks for the Italian.   Let's go.

English	Italian
city	città
university	università
possibility	possibilità
opportunity	opportunità
verity	verità
society	_____
necessity	_____

Miniquiz 2.   Now you will be given three groups of three English infinitives and the Italian equivalents for two of them. The members of each group belong to the same family, as will be obvious upon inspection.   Your job is to guess the missing Italian infinitives.

English	Italian
to admit	ammettere
to transmit	trasmettere
to permit	_____
to deduce	dedurre
to produce	produrre
to seduce	_____
to compose	comporre
to impose	imporre
to oppose	_____

Miniquiz 3.   Here you will be given five infinitives, in both English and Italian, and the Italian past participles for three of them.   Your job is to guess at the two missing participles.

You may be far enough along in your formal study to recognize that these participles are irregular; that is, they do not follow the usual rules for Italian infinitives ending in **-ere**, those of the second conjugation.   But that really doesn't make any difference, because there is enough of a pattern here to allow you to guess at the participles, whether they are regular or not. The important thing is to look at the endings (in boldface type) of the infinitives and participles to figure out the pattern. Take a crack at it!

English Infinitive	Italian Infinitive	Italian Past Participle
to depict, paint	dipin**gere**	dipin**to**
to push	spin**gere**	spin**to**
to dye, tint	tin**gere**	tin**to**
to function	fun**gere**	_____
to feign, pretend	fin**gere**	_____

Now check your work against the answers below and on page 4.

Answers to the Miniquizzes

Answers for Miniquiz 1. The basic pattern for the words in Miniquiz 1 is that English words ending in -ty usually end in -tà in Italian. Therefore the answers are as follows:

English	Italian
city	città
university	università
possibility	possibilità
opportunity	opportunità
verity	verità
society	società
necessity	necessità

Answers for Miniquiz 2. The patterns here are that English verbs ending in -mit usually correspond with Italian verbs ending in -mettere; similarly, -duce goes with -durre and -pose with -porre.

to admit	am**mettere**
to transmit	tras**mettere**
to permit	per**mettere**
to deduce	de**durre**
to produce	pro**durre**
to seduce	se**durre**
to compose	com**porre**
to impose	im**porre**
to oppose	op**porre**

Reflections on the Miniquizzes

How did you do on the three miniquizzes? If you got all the answers correct, you should excel at the kinds of pattern recognition used in many places in this book. If you made mistakes, but then on thinking about the patterns and examples given in the answers, the principles became clear to you, you will still be able to use the pattern-recognition idea to good advantage. You are well on your way to becoming an Educated Guesser.

The Use of Cognates

Cognates are words that in two different languages resemble each other in spelling, pronunciation, and meaning (a topic we discuss in detail in a later chapter). We made use of cognates in the three miniquizzes you just took, and we are sure you saw many resemblances.

Undoubtedly you saw (or can see now, after your attention has been called to it), resemblances in such word pairings as the following:

English	Italian
university	università
possibility	possibilità
to admit	ammettere
to produce	produrre
to depict	dipingere
to tint	tingere

Answers to the Miniquizzes (continued)

Answers to Miniquiz 3. The pattern here is that Italian infinitives ending in **-gere** have participles ending in **-to**. There are some exceptions to the rule, as you will see in Chapter 6, "Faking Out Irregular Past Participles," but the rule holds up well enough to make it worth learning.

English Infinitive	Italian Infinitive	Italian Past Participle
to depict, paint	dipingere	dipinto
to push	spingere	spinto
to dye, tint	tingere	tinto
to function	fungere	funto
to feign, pretend	fingere	finto

In fact, in the three miniquizzes presented, there was only one set of words for which there was no resemblance at all between the English and the Italian. All other pairs contained at least some degree of similarity. You will find such dissimilar pairs as the following to be in the minority:

to push   spingere

Go back over the miniquizzes and note the many resemblances that are there. Those similarities should make it easier for you to remember Italian words you had never seen before. We will call your attention to such resemblances frequently throughout this book. They are another form of pattern recognition.

Welcome to the world of Educated Guessing!

HOW THIS BOOK CAN HELP YOU

Practicality of Vocabulary

We have made an effort throughout this book to introduce you to words and phrases in common use in Italy today. We learned many of them while living in Italy and seeing them in newspapers, magazines, and books, as well as hearing them in conversation and on TV. Others were taken from the frequency-of-usage lists published by Juilland and Traversa.* Some of the livelier expressions we present are not often found in traditional texts, but they are colorful and worth knowing.

Know Your Grammar

Obviously you are serious about learning to write and speak Italian well, or you would not have bought this book. You will have to know your grammar. Educated Guessing will enhance the process nicely, but you will also need to study your textbook.

At many places in this book, we describe certain grammatical points that you must understand if the material we present is to make sense and be useful to you. Our descriptions of grammar are often not as detailed and thorough as those of your text, and you should consult your text as necessary to be sure you understand the grammatical principles; our restatement of them could be

---

* Juilland, Alphonse, and Vicenzo Traversa: Frequency Dictionary of Italian Words, Mouton, The Hague, 1973, esp. pp. 405-519.

considered to be a review or a refresher. For instance, in Chapter 14, "Yesterday, Today, and Tomorrow: Expressions of Time," we introduce many expressions involving the past and the future. At that point you must know how to form and when to use at least three verb tenses in addition to the present tense: the **passato prossimo** (present perfect), the **imperfetto** (imperfect) and, for the future, the **futuro.**

Complementarity

By now you will see the complementarity between this book and your class text. Your text will provide the basic structure of the language and will teach you the many grammatical points you need to master. At the same time, this book will make it possible for you to add hundreds of words to your vocabulary, to fake out great numbers of irregular verbs without having to learn the irregularities one by one, and to find a number of expressions and idioms that will be immediately useful to you, in a very economical manner.

What we are trying to do in this book is beat the rap of rote memorization whenever possible. When such memorization is unavoidable, we provide interesting and useful expressions to make the work worthwhile.

We suggest that now you look over the introductory sections for the next several chapters, to get an idea of what each chapter deals with. Some of the chapters may be useful to you right away; if so, go ahead and read them. Others will be appropriate only after you have studied a bit more of your text, at which point you may say to yourself, "Aha! This ties in nicely with one of the chapters in Italian for Educated Guessers. Now is the time to go back to it and see what goodies I can find."

TWO

COGNATES: FAITHFUL AND QUASI

COGNATES

Faithful Cognates

Throughout this book we will systematically point out to you similarities and parallels between English and Italian, so that you can put your knowledge of one to work as you learn the other. The natural starting point for examining these similarities is a consideration of cognates.

Webster's dictionary* has several definitions for the word "cognate"; the one that concerns us here is as follows: "of a word or morpheme -- related by descent from the same root or affixal element in a recorded or assumed ancestral language." That's just a fancy way of saying that two words look alike and have similar meanings and pronunciations. Here are some examples:

benevolence	benevolenza
reproduction	riproduzione
service	servizio
treatment	trattamento
university	università

---

*Webster's Third New International Dictionary, Springfield, Mass., G. & C. Merriam Company, 1961, p. 440.

These pairs have faithful resemblances in looks, meanings, and pronunciations, so we will call them Faithful Cognates and use the abbreviation FC to identify them from time to time in this book.

Unfaithful Cognates

How about the pair **pretendere** - to pretend? In spelling they certainly are similar, but in meaning they are somewhat different. To pretend in English most often means to play an artificial role, to feign. **Pretendere** in Italian most often means to have a claim on, as in "to pretend to a throne," or "I wouldn't pretend to understand." (To feign in Italian is **fingere** or **fare finta**.) This lack of correspondence between spelling and meaning gives one a sense of betrayal, of unfaithfulness. We shall call those guilty of such infidelity Unfaithful Cognates.

We will devote a later chapter to a discussion of these troublemakers and use the abbreviation UC to identify individual examples that pop up in this book.

Quasi-Cognates

Examine these pairs of words:

the kitchen	cucina
to encounter	incontrare
the price	prezzo
to develop	sviluppare
to touch	toccare

Intuitively you can sense some similarities between the pairs, but at first it may be difficult to pin down the similarities. On reflection, with **s/vilupp/are** and de/velop/, for instance, one can see that it is the v-l-p portions of the words that are similar. Quasi-Cognates is the term we will use for such less-evident resemblances, and the abbreviation will be QC.

Cognates in This Book

In this chapter we will discuss Faithful Cognates and introduce you to some Quasi-Cognates. We won't discuss Faithful Cognates further in the book, but in later chapters you will find more Quasi-Cognates as well as Unfaithful Cognates.

Now on to a more detailed discussion of Cognates Faithful and Quasi.

FAITHFUL COGNATES

Many English words of Latin origin have Italian counterparts. There are some orderly ways in which classical Latin words have been transformed into modern English and Italian, and by knowing these parallel pathways, the Educated Guesser can often translate from one language to the other without the intervention of a dictionary.

Changes to the Feminine

There are several parallels in which English nouns with a given ending translate to feminine Italian words with similar endings. Four of these parallels will be shown immediately below. As you inspect these examples, see if you can discover the rules for the transformations for yourself before they are stated explicitly in the text; write your discoveries in the spaces provided. If you can do this, the rules will belong to you more securely than if you learn them passively.

<u>Transformations of the First Kind</u>

the city	la città
the cities	le città
the liberty	la libertà
the liberties	le libertà
the possibility	la possibilità
the possibilities	le possibilità

Rules: 1. _____

2. _____

<u>Transformations of the Second Kind</u>

the explanation	la spiegazione
the explanations	le spiegazioni
the reproduction	la riproduzione
the reproductions	le riproduzioni

Rules: 1. _____

2. _____

<u>Transformations of the Third Kind</u>

the benevolence	la benevolenza
the benevolences	le benevolenze
the frequency	la frequenza
the frequencies	le frequenze

Rules: 1. _____

      2. _____

Transformations of the Fourth Kind

      the kindness   la gentilezza
      the smallness   la piccolezza

Rule: 1. _____

Now that you have completed this brief exercise, you can check your abilities to make Educated Guesses about rules for Educated Guessing, already a second-order challenge, against the descriptions in the following sections.

Transformations of the First Kind. The first rule is that words ending in -ty in English end in -tà in Italian (and, therefore, that they are feminine). A second rule is that the ending of the noun does not change between singular and plural; it is a so-called invariant. See these further examples for these two rules:

      the affinity(ies)   l', le affinità
      the brutality(ies)   la, le brutalità
      the felicity(ies)   la, le felicità
      the liberty(ies)   la, le libertà
      the university(ies)   l', le università

Transformations of the Second Kind. The rules here are (1) that words ending in -tion in English usually end in -zione in Italian, and (2) that the Italian plural is the expected one, namely -zioni. Here are some examples:

      the aggregation(s)   l', le aggregazione(i)
      the election(s)   l', le elezione(i)
      the explanation(s)   la, le spiegazione(i)
      the reproduction(s) la, le riproduzione(i)
      the solution(s)   la, le soluzione(i)
      the station(s)   la, le stazione(i)

Transformations of the Third Kind. The rules here are (1) that English words ending in -nce or -ncy that derive from Latin usually have Italian counterparts ending in -anza or -enza, and (2) that the plurals are formed as one would expect. Note these examples:

      the arrogance(s)   l', le arroganza(e)
      the benevolence(s)   la, le benevolenza(e)
      the preference(s)   la, le preferenza(e)
      the frequency(ies)   la, le frequenza(e)

<u>Transformations of the Fourth Kind</u>. The rule here is that words ending in <u>-ness</u> in English usually end in **-ezza** in Italian. Often the first part of the word comes from the Latin, e.g. <u>abstract</u>edness - **astratt**ezza; but sometimes it comes from an Anglo-Saxon root on to which the <u>-ness</u> has been grafted, e.g. <u>kind</u>ness - **gentilezza**. Study these examples:

abstractedness	astrattezza
contentedness	contentezza
cheekiness	sfrontatezza
kindness	gentilezza
smallness	piccolezza
tallness	altezza

The Case of the Disappearing "n"

The letter "n" is part of the common prefixes (often followed by the letter "s") <u>cons-</u>, <u>ins-</u>, and <u>trans-</u>, in such English words as <u>cons</u>tant, <u>ins</u>tant, and <u>trans</u>port. Sometimes the letter "n" makes a mysterious disappearance in the equivalent Italian word; sometimes it appears as expected. It turns out that these disappearances can be made less mysterious for the Educated Guesser if we make a slight digression on the topic of the **s-impura** and how it makes "n" disappear.

<u>The s-impura</u>. The **s-impura** (an "impure s") is an "s" that starts a word or syllable and is followed by a <u>consonant</u>. (If it is followed by a <u>vowel</u>, it is NOT an **s-impura**.) In the following examples, the letter "s" and the letter following it (consonant or vowel) appear in boldface type in the Italian words.

<u>An s-impura</u>		<u>Not an s-impura</u>	
sconto	discount	**so**stanza	substance
sdegno	disdain	**se**rvire	to serve
tra**sc**rivere	transcribe	**so**stare	to stop, rest
co**st**ante	constant	tran**si**zione	transition
i**sp**irare	to inspire	tran**sa**zione	transaction

<u>The Prefix "Trans-."</u> For some reason, the English prefix <u>trans-</u> is the one most consistently affected by the "n" that disappears when it is followed by an **s-impura**, as the next five examples show. Then there are two examples where <u>trans-</u> is <u>not</u> followed by an **s-impura**; <u>trans-</u> keeps its "n."

<u>An s-impura</u>

to transcribe	trascrivere
to transfer	trasferire
transfiguration	trasfigurazione
to transmit	trasmettere
transparent	trasparente

<u>Not an s-impura</u>

transition	transizione
transaction	transazione

<u>The Prefix "Cons-."</u> Much of the same obtains for words beginning with <u>cons-</u> in English. With an **s-impura**, the "n" disappears; without it, it remains. Note these examples:

<u>An s-impura</u>

conspicuous	cospicuo
to conspire	cospirare
constant	costante
to constitute	costituire
to construct	costruire

<u>Not an s-impura</u>

conservation	conservazione
consummation	consumazione

<u>The Prefix "Ins-."</u> Things are a bit more inconsistent with the prefix **ins-**. Sometimes the "n" disappears as the rule predicts; sometimes it does not. The Educated Guesser should be aware of this case and recognize that sometimes Italian words beginning with **is-** are the equivalent of English words beginning with <u>ins-</u>, as shown in these examples:

<u>An s-impura</u>

to inspire	ispirare
institute	istituto

<u>But</u>

inspiration	inspirazione
to instill	instillare

A Few Other Transformations

We have a few more rules for transformations of Faithful Cognates and then a quiz to show you how much Italian you already know just by knowing English. We shall touch on some other rules in later chapters, but these are enough for now.

Words Ending in "-ent." Many English adjectives and nouns that end in -ent go to -ente in Italian, as shown in these examples:

evident	evidente
frequent	frequente
incident	incidente
Orient	oriente
permanent	permanente

Words with "c," "f," or "p" Followed by "l." When an English word starts with "c," "f," or "p," and it is followed by the letter "l," the Italian equivalent often replaces the "l" with an "i," as in flower - fiore. For English words starting with a hard "c," to keep the sound of "k," the Italian usually starts with chi-, as in the pair clear - chiaro. Here are some examples:

clear	chiaro
to close	chiudere
flank	fianco
Florence	Firenze
flower	fiore
plan	piano, pianta
plate	piatto

The Soft, Sweet Sound of Doubled Consonants. One reason the Italian language sounds so sweet to American ears is that Latin prefixes such as ad- and ob- are often altered so that the "d" or "b" in the prefix is changed to be the same as the first consonant of the word itself. Examples:

adjective	aggettivo
advocate	avvocato
obvious	ovvio

Similarly, many words that have a ct or a pt in English have a tt in Italian. Examples:

act	atto
conduct	condotto
conflict	conflitto
Egypt	Egitto
fact	fatto
interrupted	interrotto
protected	protetto

Thus the Educated Guesser may, as a general rule, smooth out a ct or pt in English to a tt in Italian.

<u>Peculiarities of Words Beginning with "s."</u>   Many Italian words that begin with "s" (usually **s-impura**) are antonyms to the same words without the "s." This is not a universal rule, however, as the exceptions noted below demonstrate.

to charge, load	caricare
to **dis**charge	**s**caricare
fortunate	fortunato
unfortunate	**s**fortunato
trust, faith	fiducia
mistrust	**s**fiducia
disdain	**s**degno

<u>But</u>

to dissent	dissentire
disorganized	disorganizzato
misgovernment	malgoverno
uninterrupted	ininterrotto
unintelligible	inintelligibile

From these examples, you can see that a number of English affixes that turn a word into its opposite, e.g. <u>dis-</u>, <u>un-</u>, <u>mis-</u>, convert to an **s-impura** in Italian. But many do not, as the exceptions show, so it would not be smart for one to convert to **s-impura** promiscuously. Instead, upon seeing an Italian word starting with an **s-impura**, the Educated Guesser may wonder, "Could this be the antonym to the same word starting without the **s-impura**?"

<u>Concerning "x" and "u."</u>   The letter "x" in English usually becomes either "s" or "ss" in Italian.

affi**x**	affi**ss**o
e**x**orcise	e**s**orcizzare
e**x**press	e**s**presso
o**x**ygen	o**ss**igeno
xylophone	**s**ilofono

Similarly, "u" sometimes goes to "o," and "ous" to "o," as in these examples:

cond**u**ct	cond**o**tta
conspicu**ous**	cospicu**o**
gregari**ous**	gregari**o**
marvell**ous**	meravigli**oso**
obvi**ous**	ovvi**o**
s**u**rprised	s**o**rpreso
v**u**lgar	v**o**lgare

Prequiz Summary

Soon there will be a quiz to check you on the material covered so far. Here is a summary of what has been presented; turn back to this summary as a cribsheet if you get stuck during the quiz.

<u>Changes to the Feminine</u>. Four kinds of changes were shown, as in these examples:

1. the possibil**ity**(ies)	la, le possibilit**à**
2. the lament**ation**(s)	la, le lament**azione**(i)
3. the benevol**ence**(s)	la, le benevol**enza**(e)
4. the kind**ness**(es)	la, le gentil**ezza**(e)

<u>The Case of the Disappearing "n."</u> For the English prefixes <u>cons-</u>, <u>ins-</u>, and <u>trans-</u>, the "n" often disappears in Italian when it is followed by an **s-impura**, e.g.:

co/<u>nsp</u>/-icuous   co/**sp**/icuo
tra/<u>nsc</u>/ribe   tra/**sc**/rivere.

<u>A Few Other Transformations</u>. English words that end in <u>-ent</u> usually go to **-ente** in Italian, e.g. <u>evident</u> - **evidente**.

When the first letters of English words are "c," "f," or "p" followed by "l," often they are followed instead by "i" in Italian, e.g. <u>plate</u> - **piatto**.

Certain consonants double to give Italian a soft, sweet sound, e.g. a/<u>dj</u>/e/<u>ct</u>/ive - a/**gg**/e/**tt**/ivo.

<u>Peculiarities of Words Beginning with "s."</u> Starting an already existing Italian word with **s-impura** often, but not always, converts it to its antonym, as in <u>fortunate</u> - **fortunato** to <u>un</u>fortunate - **s**fortunato.

<u>Concerning "x" and "u."</u> "X" may go to "s" and "u" or "ous" to "o," e.g. <u>affix</u> - **affisso**, <u>obvious</u> - **ovvio**.

QUIZ ON FAITHFUL COGNATES

Some English words with Faithful Cognates in Italian are given below. Fill in all the blanks and then check your work against the answers that follow.   The place in each word where one of our rules applies is in boldface type. (The Italian endings for the three verbs are supplied so that you will not have to guess at them.)

to **cl**arify	_____	(-icare)
univer**s**ality	_____	
tran**sf**ormation	_____	
con**st**ernation	_____	
bene**d**iction	_____	
immin**ence**	_____	
elec**t**ive	_____	
to tran**sc**ribe	_____	(-ivere)
mor**t**ality	_____	
(the) func**t**ion	_____	
closure	_____	
tran**s**itive	_____	
profun**d**ity	_____	
excell**ence**	_____	
Eg**yp**t	_____	
erec**t**ion	_____	
to con**s**ent	_____	(-tire)

Answers to Quiz on Faithful Cognates

Here are the answers; boldface type in both English and Italian identifies the portion of each word where the rules apply.

to **cl**arify	**chi**arificare
universa**lity**	universa**lità**
transforma**tion**	**tra**sforma**zione**
consterna**tion**	consterna**zione**
bened**iction**	bened**izione**
immin**ence**	immin**enza**
elec**tive**	elet**tivo**
to **tra**ns**c**ribe	**tra**s**c**rivere
morta**lity**	morta**lità**
(the) func**tion**	fun**zione**
closure	**chi**usura
tran**si**tive	tran**si**tivo
profun**dity**	profon**dità**
excel**lence**	eccel**lenza**
E**gy**pt	E**gi**tto
erec**tion**	ere**zione**
to **co**nsent	**co**nsentire

QUASI-COGNATES

At the beginning of the chapter we gave some examples of Quasi-Cognates -- words that are similar, but where the similarities are not as apparent as those we call Faithful Cognates. Here we present a first list of 20 Quasi-Cognates; other lists will be presented in later chapters.

The Quasi-Cognates are given in English alphabetical order. Try to get them paired off in your head as they are on paper; then, on a following page, they will be presented in random order, with blanks for you to fill in. (And on the page after that, the answers will be shown -- but don't peek ahead.)

to beat	battere
the (beef)steak	la bistecca
brief	breve
to charge	caricare
the departure	la partenza
to develop	sviluppare
the employee	l'impiegato
to encounter	incontrare
to escape	scappare
to excuse	scusare
the flower	il fiore
the kitchen	la cucina
the lake	il lago
the people	il popolo
the pleasure	piacere
the point	il punto
the price	il prezzo
the rice	il riso
the salt	il sale
to touch	toccare

Quiz on Quasi-Cognates

Supply the missing words:

to charge	_____
the flower	_____
to escape	_____
to beat	_____
the salt	_____
the lake	_____
the employee	_____
the kitchen	_____
the rice	_____
to excuse	_____

_____	toccare
_____	la bistecca
_____	incontrare
_____	il prezzo
_____	il piacere
_____	sviluppare
_____	il punto
_____	la partenza
_____	il popolo
_____	breve

to charge	**caricare**
the flower	**il fiore**
to escape	**scappare**
to beat	**battere**
the salt	**il sale**
the lake	**il lago**
the employee	**l'impiegato**
the kitchen	**la cucina**
the rice	**il riso**
to excuse	**scusare**
to touch	toccare
the (beef)steak	la bistecca
to encounter	incontrare
the price	il prezzo
the pleasure	il piacere
to develop	sviluppare
the point	il punto
the departure	la partenza
the people	il popolo
brief	breve

THREE.

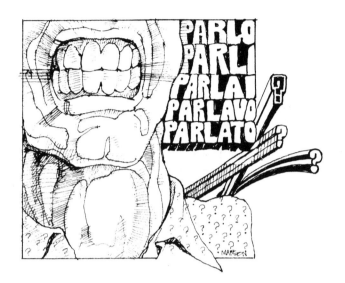

DON'T GET
TENSED UP
ABOUT
TENSES

This chapter is placed early in the book, while you are beginning to learn Italian, to help you learn to express yourself in speech and writing. In it, you will be advised to skip, for the time being, a number of tenses and verb forms in order to make life simpler. Those skipped forms are important, and in time you will learn them. But for now, peruse the material in this chapter and see how you can make an Educated Guess on how to express ideas about past, present, and future.

AN ANALYSIS

As inspection of Table 3.1 will show, when you add up all the tenses and forms for a verb conjugation, there are 95 different possible combinations of endings. Those shown are for the first conjugation, with **parlare** as a model verb. There are similar sets of endings for the **-ere** and **-ire** verbs; for the three conjugations there are 285 combinations! If you add those for **essere** and **avere**, you are approaching the 400 mark. Even those of you with near-photographic memories have better things to do with your time than memorize verb endings, so we will embark on a strategy of introducing you first to the two tenses most frequently used in Italian (both in the indicative), the **presente** and **passato prossimo** (enclosed in the box in Table 3.1). We will show you how they can be made to express a wide variety of ideas in present, past, and future.

TABLE 3.1.   TENSES AND FORMS FOR THE VERB **PARLARE**

INDICATIVO

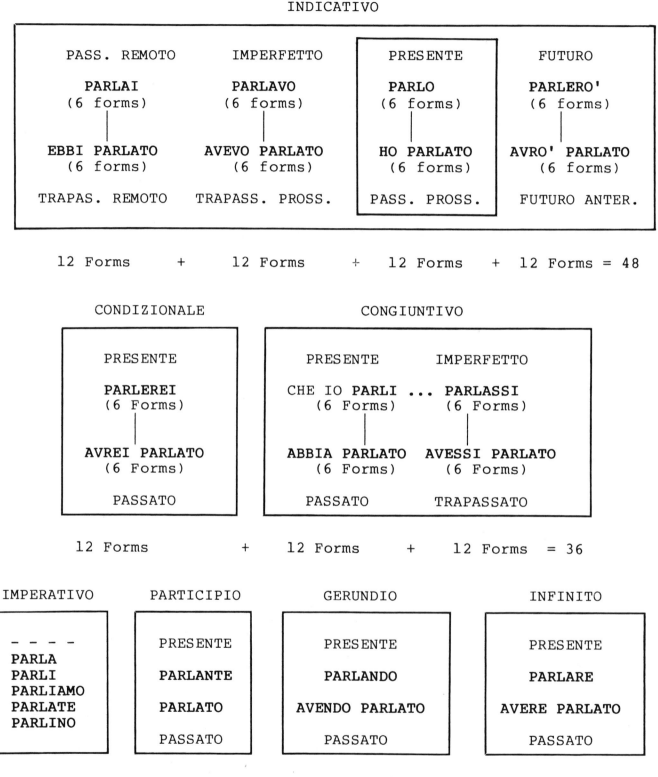

PASS. REMOTO	IMPERFETTO	PRESENTE	FUTURO
PARLAI (6 forms)	**PARLAVO** (6 forms)	**PARLO** (6 forms)	**PARLERO'** (6 forms)
EBBI PARLATO (6 forms)	**AVEVO PARLATO** (6 forms)	**HO PARLATO** (6 forms)	**AVRO' PARLATO** (6 forms)
TRAPAS. REMOTO	TRAPASS. PROSS.	PASS. PROSS.	FUTURO ANTER.

12 Forms   +   12 Forms   +   12 Forms   +   12 Forms = 48

CONDIZIONALE   CONGIUNTIVO

PRESENTE
PARLEREI (6 Forms)
AVREI PARLATO (6 Forms)
PASSATO

PRESENTE	IMPERFETTO
CHE IO **PARLI** ... **PARLASSI** (6 Forms) (6 Forms)	
ABBIA PARLATO **AVESSI PARLATO** (6 Forms) (6 Forms)	
PASSATO	TRAPASSATO

12 Forms   +   12 Forms   +   12 Forms = 36

IMPERATIVO   PARTICIPIO   GERUNDIO   INFINITO

IMPERATIVO
- - - - **PARLA** **PARLI** **PARLIAMO** **PARLATE** **PARLINO**

PARTICIPIO
PRESENTE **PARLANTE** **PARLATO** PASSATO

GERUNDIO
PRESENTE **PARLANDO** **AVENDO PARLATO** PASSATO

INFINITO
PRESENTE **PARLARE** **AVERE PARLATO** PASSATO

5 Forms   +   2 Forms   +   2 Forms   +   2 Forms = 11 Forms

Summary: 48 Forms + 36 Forms + 11 Forms = 95 Forms for **PARLARE**

At other places in the book, we will gradually introduce you to a given tense or form, as you are ready to begin using it (and, in fact, where mastery of the accompanying material makes it necessary that you be familiar with it), so that the work of mastering a few more of those 400 or so endings has some immediate payoff.

A STRATEGY

Now we will focus on two tenses in the indicative, the **presente** and the **passato prossimo**.

Our basic strategy here is based on the following two rules:

1. <u>Use the **indicativo presente** plus expressions of time to express things occurring in the present and future.</u>

Examples: I <u>go</u> to the store <u>now</u>.
                        Adesso vado al mercato.

                   I (<u>will</u>) <u>go</u> to the store <u>tomorrow</u>.
                        Domani vado al mercato.

2. <u>Use the present perfect (**passato prossimo**) plus expressions of time to express things occurring in the recent or remote past.</u>

Examples: I <u>went</u> to the store <u>yesterday</u>.
                        Ieri sono andato al mercato.

                   I <u>went</u> to the store <u>twenty years ago</u>.
                        Sono andato al mercato **venti anni fa**.

If you follow these two rules, you need learn only the present indicative endings of **essere** (to be), **avere** (to have), and the three conjugations. The **passato prossimo** is simply the present of **essere** or **avere** conjugated with the past participle of the verb. With fewer than 40 endings, you will be in business.

A SLIGHT DIGRESSION

A Little Grammar

Most grammars use the terms <u>present perfect</u> and **passato prossimo** to describe the tenses we are dealing with here, but occasionally other terms are used. To be sure we all have the same verb forms in mind, here are samples of the **passato prossimo** as it is used with **parlare** (conjugated with **avere**) and **andare** (conjugated with **essere**). We will assume that you have already learned the rules that govern the choice of **avere** or **essere**.

Parlare		Andare	
ho parlato	abbiamo parlato	sono andato	siamo andati
hai parlato	avete parlato	sei andato	siete andati
ha parlato	hanno parlato	è andato	sono andati

The Simple Past in English Leads to Perfect Italian

In English, we usually use the <u>simple past</u> to describe completed actions occurring in the past, as in this example:

> We first met John five years ago. He then went to Rome to begin a job. After two years he left Rome and came to Florence. That was the second time John came to visit us. He stayed with us for two months. He returned again two weeks ago. He ate here last night. He left for work early this morning.

In Italian, as in many European languages, the <u>present perfect</u> (**il passato prossimo**) is used for such constructions. Our example, cast in the **passato prossimo**, reads as follows:

> **Abbiamo incontrato** Gianni per la prima volta cinque anni fa. Poi **è andato** a Roma per cominciare a lavorare. Dopo due anni **è partito** da Roma ed **è venuto** a Firenze. Questa **è stata** la seconda volta che Gianni **è venuto** a trovarci. Lui **è rimasto** con noi per due mesi. Due settimane fa lui **è tornato** ancora. Ieri sera **ha cenato** qui. Stamattina presto lui **è uscito** per andare al lavoro.

Now let's translate this paragraph literally, from the Italian **passato prossimo** into the English <u>present perfect</u>.

> We have met John for the first time five years ago. Then he has gone to Rome to begin a job. After two years he has left Rome and has come to Florence. This has been the second time that John has come to visit us. He has stayed with us for two months. He has arrived again two weeks ago. He has eaten here with us last night. He has left for work early this morning.

That last paragraph is grammatically correct, but it just doesn't <u>sound</u> right. It has a stilted and stiff quality to it, as if it were a European speaking English learned in school. That's because our European was quite literally using his <u>present perfect</u> when he should have employed our <u>simple past</u>.

The point to be remembered here concerns simple narration of completed actions:

> Use the Italian <u>present perfect</u> (**passato prossimo**) to express English <u>simple past</u> constructions.

There is an <u>imperfect</u> (**imperfetto**) in Italian, but it is <u>not</u> used to describe simple completed actions. We'll discuss it in a later chapter. There are several other types of past tenses in Italian, each with its own indications for use. Later we'll tackle some of those, too.

BACK TO THE STRATEGY

Before our digression into grammar, we had suggested using the present tense to describe present and future, and using the **passato prossimo** for events of the past, using expressions of time to qualify in either case.

A Practice Session

Let's see how it works. You will occasionally be ungrammatical but always perfectly comprehensible. Below are sixteen expressions of time to use for starters. You will find a more comprehensive list in Chapter 14, "Yesterday, Today, and Tomorrow: Expressions of Time."

<u>Present and Future</u>		<u>Past</u>	
now	ora, adesso	then	allora, poi
in 5 minutes	fra 5 minuti	5 minutes ago	5 minuti fa
today	oggi	yesterday	ieri
tomorrow	domani	two days ago	due giorni fa
next week	la settimana prossima	last week	la settimana scorsa
soon	fra poco	a little while ago	poco fa
next month	il mese prossimo	last month	il mese scorso (passato)
next year	l'anno prossimo	last year	l'anno scorso (passato)

Examples

1. I <u>(will) go</u> to the store <u>tomorrow</u>.

    Vado al mercato **domani**.

2. I <u>(will) return</u> to the United States <u>next year</u>.

    Torno negli Stati Uniti **l'anno prossimo**.

3. <u>We (will) eat</u> at a restaurant tomorrow.

    Domani mangiamo al ristorante.

4. We <u>went</u> to Rome <u>last week</u>.

    Siamo andati a Roma **la settimana scorsa**.

5. He <u>came</u> to Florence <u>years ago</u>.

    Lui è venuto a Firenze **anni fa**.

6. He <u>spoke</u> here <u>yesterday</u>.

    Ha parlato qui **ieri**.

QUIZ ON TENSES

Below are eight sentences given in English. If the verb is not one we have used before, the Italian infinitive is supplied in parentheses, as well as other Italian words you may not know. Translate the English into Italian in the spaces provided, and then check your work against the answers later. (If you have forgotten an expression of time, feel free to look it up on the preceding pages.)

1. Elena will come home (a casa) next week.

   _____

2. Luigi went to Rome ten (dieci) years ago.

   _____

3. We bought (comprare) the car (la macchina) months ago.

   _____

4. Anna will go shopping (fare le spese) tomorrow.

   _____

5. The voyage (il viaggio) begins (cominciare) soon.

   _____

6. Maria arrived (arrivare) in Italy last year.

   _____

7. What (che cosa) will Piero do (fare) next week?

   _____

8. He heard (sentire) the news (le notizie) yesterday.

   _____

1. Elena will come home next week.

   Elena **viene** a casa **la settimana prossima.**

2. Luigi went to Rome ten years ago.

   Luigi **è andato** a Roma **dieci anni fa.**

3. We bought the car months ago.

   Abbiamo comprato la macchina **mesi fa.**

4. Anna will go shopping tomorrow.

   Anna **fa** le spese **domani.**

5. The voyage begins soon.

   Il viaggio **comincia fra poco.**

6. Maria arrived in Italy last year.

   Maria **è arrivata** in Italia **l'anno scorso.**

7. What will Piero do next week?

   Che cosa **fa** Piero **la settimana prossima?**

8. He heard the news yesterday.

   Lui **ha sentito** le notizie **ieri.**

FOUR.

THE
REGULARITIES
OF IRREGULAR
VERBS

Verbs can be irregular in a number of ways. Some are irregular in the way they form the present indicative (and therefore the forms that derive from it in the imperative and subjunctive). Some are irregular in the way they form their past participles.

These irregularities have to be memorized, as much of a drag as that might be, because many of these verbs are among the most frequently used in writing and speech.

Such memorization pays off. There are many parallels across cases, so that often the effort expended in learning one set of irregular endings can easily result in being able to anticipate the same set of endings for related verbs. We will call these parallels "regular irregularities." Thus, many of the verbs you encounter in this chapter are not only important for themselves, but they will also serve as prototypes for words you will encounter later. Before getting to the verbs, let's do a little groundwork, so that you will be able to see, when you start looking at the verbs, how learning them will prepare you for the later chapters.

REGULAR IRREGULARITIES

A Derivation and a Definition

We are borrowing the term "regular irregularities" from the medical specialty of cardiology. There the term applies to the situation when the heartbeat is irregular (abnormal), but in a regular fashion. For instance, the heart might have three normal beats, then drop the fourth (expected) beat, be followed by three more normal beats, then another dropped fourth beat, etc. The classification of regular irregularities leads to refined ideas about diagnosis and treatment of certain heart conditions.

In this book, we will define a "regular irregularity" as one that, when learned for one verb, can be applied correctly in the same manner for related or similar verbs. We will point out the irregularities and the relationships as we go along, so that as you are learning the irregularity, you will also see where else it applies.

It would be nice if all irregularities were regular -- that is, had further applications. Unfortunately, such is not the case. Some irregular verbs must be learned just for themselves, where there will be no transfer of learning. So be it. But where the possibility of transfer of learning exists, we will point it out to you.

Kinds of Regular Irregularities

In the Present Indicative. The usual rule is that, for each of the conjugations, one derives the six forms (three singular, three plural) by lopping off the end of the infinitive and adding the proper endings, as shown here:

Parlare	Credere	Dormire
parl/o	cred/o	dorm/o
parl/i	cred/i	dorm/i
parl/a	cred/e	dorm/e
parl/iamo	cred/iamo	dorm/iamo
parl/ate	cred/ete	dorm/ite
parl/ano	cred/ono	dorm/ono

But then we encounter **finire**, which has an unforeseen **-isc-** stem in four of its six forms, as we see here:

Finire: To Finish

fin**isc**o	finiamo
fin**isc**i	finite
fin**isc**e	fin**isc**ono

Other verbs have a similar or identical stem; we will be taking a look at them soon.

Verb Families: In the Present Tense. Many verbs are members of families (an idea covered in detail in a later chapter), where an irregularity of the root verb in the present is repeated faithfully by all family members. Later we will look at the irregular present of **tenere** (to keep, hold) and see how such other family members as **mantenere** (to maintain), **contenere** (to contain), etc., follow the same pattern.

Verb Families: The Past Participles. Similarly, when the root verb of a family is irregular in forming its past participle, the family members nearly always follow the same pattern.

The past participle of **mettere** (to place) is **messo**, not the expected **mettuto**. There are nearly twenty members of the **mettere** family, e.g. **ammettere** (to admit), **scommettere** (to bet), **sottomettere** (to submit), etc., and each one of their past participles ends in **-messo**. We will get to all of them in a later chapter, but we wanted to let you in on this kind of regular irregularity here. Now let's look at verbs irregular in the present.

VERBS IRREGULAR IN THE PRESENT: A FIRST GO-ROUND

The "-isco" Verbs

Let's take a look at the present tense of **finire** again.

Finire: To Finish

fin**isco**	finiamo
fin**isci**	finite
fin**isce**	fin**iscono**

The **-isc-** stem appears in all three singular forms and the in third person plural. Verbs with this kind of irregularity are often referred to as "**-isco**" verbs.

The verbs **capire** (to understand) and **preferire** (to prefer) are conjugated in the same way. There will be a quiz on them soon.

Two other verbs whose infinitives end in **-ire**, **uscire** (to exit, go out) and **riuscire** (to manage to, to succeed at), have present tenses that are quite similar to **finire**, except that an "e" is in the stem of the **-sc-** forms instead of an "i." Look them over until you think you have learned them.

Uscire: To Go Out

esco	usciamo
esci	uscite
esce	escono

Riuscire: To Succeed At

riesco	riusciamo
riesci	riuscite
riesce	riescono

Finally for this group, two more verbs, with infinitives this time ending in **-ere**, are conjugated like **-isco** verbs, namely **conoscere** (to know someone or some place) and **riconoscere** (to recognize someone or something). They are frequently used and you should be familiar with them. (The Latin word common in English, **cognoscenti** -- those in the know -- is a Faithful Cognate of **conoscere**, as is <u>recognize</u> for **riconoscere**.)

Conoscere: To Know		Riconoscere: To Recognize	
conosco	conosciamo	riconosco	riconosciamo
conosci	conoscete	riconosci	riconoscete
conosce	conoscono	riconosce	riconoscono

A Quiz on "**-isco**" Verbs

Review the following verbs to be sure you know their meanings and how to form them: **capire, conoscere, finire, preferire, riconoscere, riuscire,** and **uscire**. Then write translations of the words and phrases in the spaces provided below. Answers are on page 34.

1. he succeeds at

    _____

2. they recognize

    _____

3. I understand

    _____

4. you (sing.) finish

    _____

5. we prefer

    _____

6. he goes out

    _____

7. I know Florence

    _____

8. **finiamo**

    _____

9. **riconosci**

    _____

10. **escono**

    _____

11. **riesco**

    _____

12. **Lei preferisce**

    _____

13. **conoscete Piero**

    _____

14. **capiamo**

    _____

The Intrusive "g"

We have given the name of the <u>intrusive "g"</u> to the phenomenon of finding the letter "g" totally unexpectedly in the first person singular and third person plural of certain verbs. Here is an example of this surprising phenomenon:

<u>**Tenere:** To Keep, Hold</u>

tengo	teniamo
tieni	tenete
tiene	tengono

The intrusive "g" is present also in all the other members of this family, including **mantenere** (to maintain, FC), **ottenere** (to obtain, FC), etc., all of whom we will meet in a later chapter.

The intrusive "g" appears also in one of the most frequently used Italian verbs, **venire**, as shown:

<u>**Venire:** To Come</u>

vengo	veniamo
vieni	venite
viene	vengono

The intrusive "g" pops up unpredictably in many other verbs, among them **trarre** (to pull, draw), **valere** (to be worth), **scegliere** (to select), etc. In all cases where it appears in the indicative, it also appears in the imperative and present subjunctive tenses (both of them topics of later chapters). So if you get good at spotting the intrusive "g" now, you will be better able to make an Educated Guess when you start forming imperatives and subjunctives.

As you can see from this material on **-isco-** verbs and those with an intrusive "g," the irregularities extend to family members. It is more economical to learn these regular irregularities when you study the families, so that what you learn for the main verbs can be applied immediately to the other family members. Thus we will defer any further discussion of regular irregularities to the chapters dealing with verb families, starting with the next chapter.

The remainder of this chapter will deal with "<u>irregular</u> irregularities."

IRREGULAR IRREGULARITIES

We defined "irregular irregularities" as ones that apply only to the verb in question and cannot be extended to others. The verbs **essere** and **avere**, which you know already, are the two most widely used of such verbs.

Thus the verbs we are about to present, all of which are widely used, must be memorized, odious though that may be. Let's get on with it.

The Auxiliary Verbs

The verbs **dovere**, **potere**, and **volere** are <u>auxiliary verbs</u>. Rarely used by themselves, they are almost always used with another verb. Now is a good time to master them.

Answers to Quiz on "-isco" Verbs

1. he succeeds at
   riesce

2. they recognize
   riconoscono

3. I understand
   capisco

4. you (sing.) finish
   finisci

5. we prefer
   preferiamo

6. he goes out
   esce

7. I know Florence
   conosco Firenze

8. **finiamo**
   <u>we finish</u>

9. **riconosci**
   <u>you (sing.) recognize</u>

10. **escono**
    <u>they go out, exit</u>

11. **riesco**
    <u>I succeed at, manage to</u>

12. **Lei preferisce**
    <u>She (you, formal) prefers</u>

13. **conoscete Piero**
    <u>you (plural) know Piero</u>

14. **capiamo**
    <u>we understand</u>

Dovere: Must, To Have To. In English we say, "You <u>must</u> (<u>have to</u>) <u>do</u> something, <u>go</u> somewhere, <u>see</u> this movie," etc. The word <u>must</u> serves as an auxiliary to the words <u>do</u>, <u>go</u>, <u>see</u>. The verb **dovere** is used in the same way and, as in English, the verb it serves follows it immediately in the word order. Note this example:

Devi studiare i libri.
You <u>must</u> (<u>have to</u>) <u>study</u> the books.

Here is the verb in the present tense:

devo	dobbiamo
devi	dovete
deve	devono

Potere: Can, To Be Able To. * **Potere** means <u>can</u>, <u>to be able to</u> ("potent" is a FC). Note this example:

Lui **può andare** fuori.
He <u>can</u> (<u>is able to</u>) <u>go</u> outside.

Here is the present tense of **potere**.

posso	possiamo
puoi	potete
può	possono

Volere: To Want, Wish. **Volere** means <u>to want, wish</u> ("volition" is a FC). Note these examples:

Voglio andare a casa.
I <u>want to go</u> home.

Vuole il libro.
He <u>wants</u> the book.

---

* In English, between the verbs <u>can</u> and <u>may</u>, a wide variety of being <u>able to do</u> things can be expressed. These include having permission ("The doctor says I can ski again"; "My parents say I may go to the party"); knowing how to do or having the capacity to do something ("I can speak Italian"); being successful at or managing to accomplish something ("I can get good grades this term.")

In Italian, the verb **potere** is pretty much restricted to having the permission or possibility of doing something, e.g. **Lui può sciare** means he has permission to go skiing, but if you want to say he <u>knows</u> how to ski, you use **sapere**, e.g. "lui **sa** sciare," or if you want to say he <u>succeeds at</u> skiing, you use **riuscire**, e.g. "lui **riesce** a sciare."

The present tense of **volere** contains the intrusive "g"
<u>three</u> times, as we shall see.

voglio	vogliamo
vuoi	volete
vuole	vogliono

The Remainder

We will shortly list the rest of the irregulars. We have
chosen five very frequently used ones, thus making it important to
know them. We will make a brief comment about each one and then
give its conjugation in the present.

<u>**Bere**</u>: To Drink. This is a contraction of the Latin
bevere (from which our word "beverage" is derived). That is why
the **bev-** stem appears in all of its forms, even though it is not
present in the infinitive.

bevo	beviamo
bevi	bevete
beve	bevono

<u>**Dare**</u>: To Give. In addition to the conventional meaning
of giving gifts, it sometimes is used to indicate conferring a
quality, e.g. **"Il televisore ti dà fastidio?"** ("Does the
television bother you -- give you bother?")

do	diamo
dai	date
dà	danno

<u>**Fare**</u>: To Make, Do. This verb, derived from the Latin
facere, is <u>one of the most widely used of all Italian verbs</u>.
Because of its Latin infinitive, the stem **fac-** is often seen in
its various forms.

faccio	facciamo
fai	fate
fa	fanno

<u>**Sapere**</u>: To Know (Something).

so	sappiamo
sai	sapete
sa	sanno

You must be careful to distinguish the kinds of knowing denoted by **sapere** from those of **conoscere**. **Sapere** means to know something or know how to do something, as in these examples:

Sai che lui arriva? <u>Do</u> you <u>know</u> that he's arriving?

Lui **sa** leggere. He <u>knows</u> (<u>how to</u>) read.

In contrast, **conoscere** means to know or to be familiar with a person or a place -- to know, for instance, Lorenzo the Magnificent or to know Genoa.

<u>Stare: To Be, Stand</u>. To the common greeting, **"Come stai?"** ("How are you?"), respond, as do the Florentines, **"Non c'è male."** ("Not bad").

sto	stiamo
stai	state
sta	stanno

QUIZ ON IRREGULAR IRREGULARITIES

Fill in the blanks, then check against answers on page 38.

English	Italian	English	Italian
1. We go _____		14. We stand, are _____	
2. I understand _____		15. I prefer _____	
3. They exit _____		16. We give _____	
4. He can _____		17. He exits _____	
5. You (pl.) give _____		18. I recognize _____	
6. We want _____		19. You (sing.) must _____	
7. You (sing.) are _____		20. He knows (someone) _____	
8. He understands _____		21. You (pl.) have _____	
9. You (sing.) do _____		22. They keep _____	
10. They come _____		23. We know (something) _____	
11. We succeed at _____		24. He gives _____	
12. You (pl.) drink _____		25. They go _____	
13. They make, do _____		26. She finishes _____	

Answers to Quiz on Irregular Irregularities

1.	We go	**andiamo**	14.	We stand, are	**stiamo**
2.	I understand	**capisco**	15.	I prefer	**preferisco**
3.	They exit	**escono**	16.	We give	**diamo**
4.	He can	**può**	17.	He exits	**esce**
5.	You (pl.) give	**date**	18.	I recognize	**riconosco**
6.	We want	**vogliamo**	19.	You (sing.) must	**devi**
7.	You (sing.) are	**stai, sei**	20.	He knows (John)	**conosce**
8.	He understands	**capisce**	21.	You (pl.) have	**avete**
9.	You (sing.) do	**fai**	22.	They keep	**tengono**
10.	They come	**vengono**	23.	We know (a fact)	**sappiamo**
11.	We succeed at	**riusciamo**	24.	He gives	**dà**
12.	You (pl.) drink	**bevete**	25.	They go	**vanno**
13.	They make, do	**fanno**	26.	She finishes	**finisce**

FIVE.

VERBS AND THEIR FAMILIES: A FIRST APPROXIMATION

WHY STUDY VERBS AND THEIR FAMILIES?

There are many economies in studying verbs as members of families. A root verb, by the addition of various prefixes, may spawn a family of five, ten, or even more verbs. By learning the root verb and adding the minimal effort it takes to apply prefixes already familiar to you in their English forms, you can learn five or ten verbs for little more than the mental price of learning one.

Regular Irregularities

In the Present Tense. When the root verb is irregular in the present tense, the family members are almost always irregular in the same way, as we have already seen for **tenere** and **mantenere, sostenere** and other family members. In all of them, the intrusive "g" was present.

In Forming the Past Participle. When the root verb is irregular in forming its past participle, the family members are almost always irregular in the same way, as we have already seen for **mettere - messo** and the family members **ammettere - ammesso; scommettere - scommesso.**

It turns out that knowing these past participles is very important, above and beyond being able to put these verbs into the **passato prossimo** easily. It is important for these two reasons:

1. Very often the English cognate or the related English word is more similar to the Italian past participle than it is to the infinitive.

2. Very often the Italian noun derived from the verb comes from the past participle, not the infinitive -- something we will expand on in a later chapter.

It turns out, too, that there are some regular irregularities in forming many of these past participles (no, they don't have to be learned one-by-one). We will explore these in the next chapter, "Faking Out Irregular Past Participles."

Cognates and Related English Words

Below we will start listing verbs, giving their Italian infinitives and past participles, their English meanings, and related English words, many of which are cognates, to help you with a reverse kind of learning. When you see the English, you will often be able to translate from English into Italian from the similarities rather than have to learn the Italian **di nuovo**.

METTERE: A SAMPLE FAMILY

The family of **mettere** is a big and useful one. Its conjugation in the present is regular; most of its members have English counterparts or cognates. The family is listed in Table 5.1.

Look Table 5.1 over carefully now, and see what kinds of parallels and similarities, i.e. what kinds of patterns, you can make out of its content. Look particularly at the following relationships and jot down in the blanks below what you think you have found:

1. Between the Italian infinitive and the Italian past

participle: _____

2. Between the the Italian infinitive and the English

infinitive: _____

3. Between either of the Italian forms and the related

English word: _____

Check your observations against the information on the page following the table.

TABLE 5.1: THE **METTERE** FAMILY

Italian Infinitive	Italian Past Participle	English Infinitive	Related English Word
mettere	messo	to place, put	missive
ammettere	ammesso	to admit	admission
commettere	commesso	to commit	commission
compromettere	compromesso	to compromise	compromise
dimetter(si)	dimesso	to resign	dismissal
immettere	immesso	to let in	(none)
intromettere	intromesso	to insert, intrude	intromission
omettere	omesso	to omit	omission
permettere	permesso	to permit	permission
premettere	premesso	to place before	premise
promettere	promesso	to promise	promise
rimettere	rimesso	to remit	remission
riprometter(si)	ripromesso	to propose	(none)
scommettere	scommesso	to bet	(none)
smettere	smesso	to stop, cease	(none)
sottometter(si)	sottomesso	to submit	submission
trasmettere	trasmesso	to transmit	transmission

Here are some of the patterns you may have detected.

1. Between the Italian infinitive and the Italian past participle: In each case, the **-mettere** of the infinitive becomes **-messo** in the participle.

2. Between the the Italian infinitive and the English infinitive: In nearly all cases, the **-mett-** of the Italian corresponds to <u>-mit</u> in the English.

3. Between either of the Italian forms and the related English Word: In virtually all cases, the English word (noun) ends in <u>-mission</u>, coming from the past participle, **-messo**, rather than the Italian infinitive.

We listed 17 members of the **mettere** family in Table 5.1, but we carefully left one out to give you a miniquiz. Inspect the word **emesso** and then answer the following questions:

1. What part of speech is it?   _____

2. What is its Italian infinitive?   _____

3. What is its English infinitive?   _____

4. What is the corresponding English noun?   _____

5. We haven't even touched on this yet, but make an Educated

Guess: What is the corresponding Italian noun?   _____

The answers are on page 43.

Prefixes

More than 20 prefixes have come over from Latin into Italian and English. Some of them are used to form large verb families, as we have seen with **mettere**; many smaller families exist, too, as we will see later in the chapter. The Latin and Italian prefixes are shown with sample Italian and English words in Table 5.2.

TABLE 5.2: LATIN AND ITALIAN PREFIXES AND EXAMPLES

Latin Prefix	Italian Prefix	Italian Example	Related English Example
ab	a + consonant	assolvere	to absolve
ad	a + consonant	ammettere	to admit
con	co + consonant	commettere	to commit
compro	compro	compromettere	to compromise
contro	contra	contravvenire	to contravene
de	de	decidere	to decide
e	e	emettere	to emit
ex	(e)s	estendere	to extend
		stendere	to hang, extend
extra	stra	stracuocere	to overcook
in	in or	iscrivere	to inscribe
	i + consonant		
intro	intro	intromettere	intromission
o, ob	o + consonant	ottenere	to obtain
per	per	permettere	to permit
pre	pre	premettere	to place before
pro	pro	promettere	to promise
re	ri	rimettere	to remit
sub	sotto	sottomettere	to submit
super	sopra, sovr	sovrintendere	to superintend
trans	tra	trafiggere	to transfix
	trans	transigere	to transact
	tras	trasmettere	to transmit
ultra	ultra	ultrasuono	ultrasound

Now you have looked at the prefixes and have an idea of the kinds of families they can spawn. The **mettere** family is one of the largest in the language, and it provided a large number of Faithful Cognates. We will look at some smaller families, not all of which provide such a high proportion of Faithful Cognates.

Answers to the Miniquiz about emesso

1. What part of speech is it?   A past participle

2. What is its Italian Infinitive?   emettere

3. What is its English Infinitive?   to emit

4. What is the corresponding English Noun?   emission

5. What is the corresponding Italian noun?   **emissione**

EIGHT MORE VERB FAMILIES

Below we will present eight more verb families. Each time we will first present the <u>infinitive</u> of the root verb with the conjugation of the <u>present tense</u>. Then we will list family members, using the same four-column format we used for **mettere**.

Each of these eight families has an average of about eight members, so you will be learning about 64 verbs for the mental price of many fewer. The verbs whose families we are presenting are these: **condurre, correre, muovere, porre, premere, tendere, tenere,** and **trarre.**

A quiz will follow.

Condurre: To Conduct

conduco	conduciamo
conduci	conducete
conduce	conducono

Italian Infinitive	Italian Past Participle	English Infinitive	Related English Word
condurre	condotto	to conduct, lead	conduction
addurre	addotto	to adduce	adduction
dedurre	dedotto	to deduce, deduct	deduction
indurre	indotto	to induce	induction
introdurre	introdotto	to introduce	introduction
produrre	prodotto	to produce	production
ridurre	ridotto	to reduce	reduction
sedurre	sedotto	to seduce	seduction
tradurre	tradotto	to translate	traduce (UC)

The Latin infinitive of **condurre** is <u>conducere</u>, which explains why the letter "c" is in the stem of all six forms of the present tense for all members of the family.

What a nice family! The English noun comes from the Italian past participle in that **-dotto** goes to <u>-duction</u> in all but one case; this is another example of "The Soft, Sweet Sound of Doubled Consonants." The one exception, **tradurre**, is the only Unfaithful Cognate of what is an otherwise extremely Faithful family.

Correre: To Run

```
corro      corriamo
corri      correte
corre      corrono
```

Italian Infinitive	Italian Past Participle	English Infinitive	Related English Word
correre	corso	to run	to course, courier
accorrere	accorso	to run, rush	(none)
concorrere	concorso	to concur, compete	concourse
discorrere	discorso	to discourse, chat	discourse
occorrere	occorso	to be necessary	occur (UC)
ricorrere	ricorso	to recur, have recourse to	recurrence
rincorrere	rincorso	to pursue	(none)
soccorrere	soccorso	to succor, help	succor
trascorrere	trascorso	to pass time	(none)

Once again we will note that **occorrere** usually means "to be necessary"; it only rarely means "to happen" (which is **succedere, accadere,** or **capitare**).

Italian ambulances and hospital emergency rooms have the words **Pronto Soccorso** on their signs: Ready First Aid.

Muovere: To Move

```
muovo      moviamo
muovi      movete
muove      muovono
```

Italian Infinitive	Italian Past Participle	English Infinitive	Related English Word
muovere	mosso	to move, stir	motion (QC)
commuovere	commosso	to move emotionally	commotion (UC)
promuovere	promosso	to promote	promotion
rimuovere	rimosso	to move again	to remove (UC)
smuovere	smosso	to shift, move	(none)
sommuovere	sommosso	to stir up, rouse	(none)

All these verbs are <u>intransitive</u>; they do <u>not</u> take an object. In English, we often use the verb <u>to move</u> as a transitive, as in: He <u>moved his furniture</u> to the apartment. The transitive Italian verb for such a case is **trasferire** (to transfer something), as in: Lui **ha trasferito** i mobili all'appartamento. (It also exists as a reflexive: Lui **si è trasferito** i mobili all'appartamento.)

This isn't a particularly good family so far as Faithful Cognates go, as you can see. One place where one of the members is frequently used in Italy is on weather maps: when you read the sea is predicted to be **poco mosso** (little motion), one can expect calm waters.

Porre: To Put, Place

pongo	poniamo
poni	ponete
pone	pongono

Italian Infinitive	Italian Past Participle	English Infinitive	Related English Word
porre	posto	to put, place	post (in place)
comporre	composto	to compose	composition
disporre	disposto	to dispose, arrange	disposition
esporre	esposto	to expose	exposition
frapporre	frapposto	to interpose	(none)
imporre	imposto	to impose	imposition
opporre	opposto	to oppose	opposition
posporre	posposto	to postpone,	postponement
proporre	proposto	to propose	proposition
riporre	riposto	to put back, away	repose (QC)
scomporre	scomposto	to decompose	decomposition
sottoporre	sottoposto	to submit	(none)
supporre	supposto	to suppose	supposition
trasporre	trasposto	to transpose	transposition

Note the intrusive "g" in the present for **porre**; it holds true for the entire family. Otherwise it is another nice family! Loads of Faithful Cognates in which the **-posto** of the Italian past participle converts to a <u>-pose</u> in the English infinitive.

Premere: To Press

```
            premo       premiamo
            premi       premete
            preme       premono
```

Italian Infinitive	Italian Past Participle	English Infinitive	Related English Word
premere	premuto	to press	(none)
comprimere	compresso	to compress	compression
deprimere	depresso	to depress	depression
esprimere	espresso	to express	expression
imprimere	impresso	to impress	impression
opprimere	oppresso	to oppress	oppression
reprimere	represso	to repress	repression
spremere	spremuto (sic!)	to squeeze out	express (med.)
sopprimere	soppresso	to suppress	suppression

Please note that the root verb, **premere**, has a regular past participle, **premuto**. Only one member of the family follows suit, **spremere - spremuto**; all others end in **-presso**. Remembering the exception can be useful, because the noun deriving from it, **la spremuta**, means the squeezing, and when you are hot and thirsty and get your requested **spremuta di arancia** (freshly squeezed orange juice), it will all have been worthwhile.

Several members of this family pop up in medical lingo. Pills or tablets from the pharmacy are called **compresse**. People who are feeling low are **depressi**. To express in American medicine can mean to squeeze out, as discharge forced from a wound.

Tendere: To Stretch, Tighten

```
            tendo       tendiamo
            tendi       tendete
            tende       tendono
```

Italian Infinitive	Italian Past Participle	English Infinitive	Related English Word
tendere	teso	to stretch, tighten	tension
attendere	atteso	to await, expect	to attend (UC)
contendere	conteso	to contend	contention
distendere	disteso	to distend	distension
estendere	esteso	to extend	extension

Italian Infinitive	Italian Past Participle	English Infinitive	Related English Word
intendere	inteso	to understand	to intend (UC)
ottendere	otteso	to obtend	to obtend (geometry)
pretendere	preteso	to claim	pretext, to pretend (UC)
protendere	proteso	to stretch out	(none)
sovrintendere	sovrinteso	to superintend	superintend
stendere	steso	to hang, extend	to extend

Beware the UC's in this family. Otherwise, it's pretty straightforward.

Tenere: To Keep, Hold

tengo	teniamo
tieni	tenete
tiene	tengono

Italian Infinitive	Italian Past Participle	English Infinitive	Related English Word
tenere	tenuto	to keep, hold	tenacious
appartenere	appartenuto	to belong (to)	appertain (UC)
attenersi	attenuto	to stick with	attain (UC)
contenere	contenuto	to contain	containment contents
detenere	detenuto	to detain	detainment
mantenere	mantenuto	to maintain	maintain
ottenere	ottenuto	to obtain	obtain
ritenere	ritenuto	to retain a point of view	retain (poss. UC)
sostenere	sostenuto	to support, hold up	sustain (poss. UC)
trattenere	trattenuto	to detain, hold back	(none)

Note the presense of the instrusive "g." Note also the possible UC situations here and be careful when you use those verbs. Here are some correct usages that may give you a feel for them:

Lui **appartiene alla** società. He <u>belongs to</u> the society.

Attenersi alle istruzioni! <u>Stick with</u> the instructions.

Se non lo **sostieni**, cade. If you don't <u>hold him up</u>, he falls.

Trarre: To Draw, Pull

```
           traggo      traiamo
           trai        traete
           trae        traggono
```

Italian Infinitive	Italian Past Participle	English Infinitive	Related English Word
trarre	tratto	to draw, pull	traction
astrarre	astratto	to abstract	abstraction
attrarre	attratto	to attract, draw	attraction
contrarre	contratto	to contract	contraction
detrarre	detratto	to detract, deduct	detract
distrarre	distratto	to distract, entertain	distraction
estrarre	estratto	to extract	extraction
protrarre	protratto	to protract, prolong	protacted
ritrarre	ritratto	to retract, deal with something again	retraction
sottrarre	sottratto	to subtract, steal	subtraction

Note the <u>double</u> intrusive "g" in the present tense.

Otherwise, another nice family! Not a UC among the ten of them; each has a Faithful Cognate. And they demonstrate the rule of "The Soft, Sweet Sounds of Doubled Consonants" in the relation-ship between **-tratto** and <u>-tract</u>.

QUIZ ON VERB FAMILIES

You know how to do this now. Fill in the blanks and then check your answers against those on the next page.

Italian Infinitive	Italian Past Participle	English Infinitive	Related English Word
introdurre	_____	_____	_____
ricorrere	_____	_____	_____
esprimere	_____	_____	_____
muovere	_____	_____	_____
_____	appartenuto	_____	_____
_____	astratto	_____	_____
_____	supposto	_____	_____
_____	ridotto	_____	_____
_____	_____	to permit	_____
_____	_____	to impose	_____
_____	_____	to depress	_____
_____	_____	to contain	_____
_____	_____	_____	distraction
_____	_____	_____	conduct
_____	_____	_____	concourse
_____	_____	_____	obtain

Answers to Quiz on Verb Families

Italian Infinitive	Italian Past Participle	English Infinitive	Related English Word
introdurre	introdotto	to introduce	introduction
ricorrere	ricorso	to recur	recourse, recurrence
esprimere	espresso	to express	expression
muovere	mosso	to move	motion
appartenere	appartenuto	to belong to	appertain (UC)
astrarre	astratto	to abstract	abstraction
supporre	supposto	to suppose	supposition
ridurre	ridotto	to reduce	reduction
permettere	permesso	to permit	permission
imporre	imposto	to impose	imposition
deprimere	depresso	to depress	depression
contenere	contenuto	to contain	containment, contents
distrarre	distratto	to distract	distraction
condurre	condotto	to conduct	conduct
concorrere	concorso	to concur, compete	concourse, concurrence
ottenere	ottenuto	to obtain	obtain

SIX.

FAKING OUT IRREGULAR PAST PARTICIPLES

Verbs of the first and third conjugations are generally quite regular in forming their past participles, so we won't worry further about them here. It is the miscreants of the second conjugation to which this chapter is devoted.

Second conjugation verbs, those ending in **-ere**, regularly form a past participle ending in **-uto**, as in **credere - creduto**. That is all very fine until exceptions start popping up, and pop up they do! Already you have encountered **mettere - messo, attendere - atteso, correre - corso**.

At times, in fact, it almost seems that the irregulars outnumber the regulars and, at first blush, the irregulars would have to be memorized one-by-one. Relief is in sight: There is a good deal more regular irregularity among second conjugation past participles than you might expect.

TWO RULES

Two rules will help the Educated Guesser figure out irregular past participles for over 150 verbs. There are occasional exceptions to the rules, but for the most part they work very well.

As we have done elsewhere, we will give you an opportunity to figure out the rules yourself, before presenting them. Below you will find a series of infinitives and past participles; inspect them and try to figure out Rule 1.

Rule 1: Verbs Ending in "-dere"

Here is a list of verbs whose infinitives end in **-dere** or **-ndere**; both the full infinitive and its ending are listed, as is the past participle for each. Can you discover a rule that governs the transformation of the infinitive to the past participle? Jot down your thoughts in the space provided.

Infinitive	Ending	Past Participle
evadere	-adere	evaso
ridere	-idere	riso
deludere	-udere	deluso
prendere	-endere	preso
confondere	-ondere	confuso

I think Rule 1 is: _____

_____

Miniquiz on Rule 1. Apply your surmise about Rule 1 to the verbs listed below. Fill in the blanks and then check your work against the statement of Rule 1 and the answers to this miniquiz on page 55.

Infinitive	Past Participle
uccidere	_____
deludere	_____
rendere	_____
spendere	_____
accendere	_____
succedere	_____

This is Rule 1: Verbs ending in **-dere** or
-ndere in the infinitive lose that ending
and generally have it replaced by <u>stem</u> +
so, e.g. eva/**dere** - eva/**so**. The vowel
of the stem changes only occasionally,
e.g. conf<u>o</u>ndere - conf<u>u</u>so.

Rule 2: Verbs Ending in "**-gere**"

Again, you have an opportunity to discover Rule 2 for
yourself. It applies to verbs ending in **-gere** and **-ggere**.
Inspect the list that follows and write down your Educated Guess
at the rule.

Infinitive	Ending	Past Participle
fingere	-gere	finto
giungere	-gere	giunto
spargere	-gere	sparso
affiggere	-ggere	affisso
leggere	-ggere	letto

I think Rule 2 is: _____

_____

Answers to Miniquiz on Rule 1

Infinitive	Past Participle
uccidere	**ucciso**
deludere	**deluso**
rendere	**reso**
spendere	**speso**
accendere	**acceso**
succedere	**successo**

Successo has one more "s" than it was supposed to have;
this is a minor exception.

Miniquiz on Rule 2. Apply your surmise about Rule 2 to the verbs shown. Rule 2 and the answers are at the bottom of page 57.

Infinitive	Past Participle
dipingere	_____
friggere	_____
prefiggere	_____
sorgere	_____
stringere	_____
volgere	_____

How did you do on the quizzes? You should have been right or very nearly right in each case. We have noted a couple of minor exceptions to the rules, e.g. that **successo** has one more "s" in it than it should have, that **stringere** went to **stretto** rather than **strinto** as the rule would predict. Such minor exceptions are a small price to pay for the powers of prediction these rules exert for the vast majority of the verbs.

WHERE TO NOW?

Shortly we will present additional batches of verbs that follow Rules 1 and 2, both to help you nail down the principles involved as well as to acquire additional vocabulary. As usual, verbs will be grouped by families, when families exist, to help economize learning.

If we listed all the verbs we have come across that fit (over 60 for Rule 1; over 90 for Rule 2), your head would soon be swimming. Thus, we will limit ourselves in this chapter to batches that can be assimilated at one sitting. The remainder will be taken up in a later chapter in a more leisurely manner.

Now to proceed to more examples.

Rule 1, Revisited

Shortly we will list for your study the remaining verbs ending in **-endere**, grouped by family when possible. We will leave verbs ending in **-ondere**, **-adere**, **-idere**, and **-udere** for Chapter 10 (but if you get curious about one of those latter verbs before you get to that chapter, go ahead and look it up).

Study the verbs in Table 6.1, then take the quiz that follows it. Verbs in families will be grouped together; "orphans" will be separated by spaces. As a refresher, here is a restatement of Rule 1:

> This is Rule 1: Verbs ending in **-dere** or **-ndere** in the infinitive lose that ending and generally have it replaced by stem + **so**, e.g. eva/**dere** - eva/**so**. The vowel of the stem changes only occasionally, e.g. conf**o**ndere - conf**u**so.

Rule 2 and Answers to Its Miniquiz

> This is Rule 2: Verbs ending in **-gere** or **-ggere** drop the ending and usually have it replaced by **-to** and **-tto**, respectively, e.g. fin/**gere** - fin/**to**; le/**ggere** - le/**tto**. For a few verbs, the participle ends in **-so** or **-sso**, e.g. **prefiggere** - **prefisso**.

Answers to Miniquiz on Rule 2

Infinitive	Past Participle
dipingere	**dipinto**
friggere	**fritto**
prefiggere	**prefisso**
sorgere	**sorto**
stringere	**stretto**
volgere	**volto**

Stringere goes to **stretto** rather than **strinto**, another minor exception. In fact, **strinto** exists, but is rarely used. **Prefiggere** goes to **prefisso**, one of the significant minority which demonstrate this transformation.

TABLE 6.1: PARTICIPLES OF INFINITIVES ENDING IN "**-ENDERE**"

Italian Infinitive	Italian Past Participle	English Infinitive	Related English Word
accendere	acceso	to light, kindle	incendiary
ascendere	asceso	to ascend	ascent
discendere	disceso	to descend	descent
scendere	sceso	to descend	descent
fendere	fesso *	to cut, fend off	fend
difendere	difeso	to defend	defense
offendere	offeso	to offend	offense
pendere	penduto **	to hang	pending, pendant
appendere	appeso	to append, hang up	appendix
dipendere	dipeso	to depend	dependence
propendere	propeso	to be inclined	propensity
sospendere	sospeso	to suspend	suspense
prendere	preso	to take, seize	prehensile
apprendere	appreso	to learn	apprehend (UC)
comprendere	compreso	to comprise, include	comprehension
intraprendere	intrapreso	to undertake	enterprise
riprendere	ripreso	to take up again	reprise (music)
sorprendere	sorpreso	to surprise	surprise
rendere	reso	to render, give back	render
spendere	speso	to spend	spend, expense

---

* "**fesso**" is never used, I am told by Italian friends.

** Exception to Rule 1: **penduto** exists but is virtually never used; it has a regular ending, but the participles of its family members <u>are</u> used and <u>do</u> follow the rule.

TABLE 6.1 (continued)

Italian Infinitive	Italian Past Participle	English Infinitive	Related English Word
tendere	teso	to tend	tend
attendere	atteso	to await, expect	attend (UC)
contendere	conteso	to contend (for)	contention (poss. UC)
distendere	disteso	to distend	distension
estendere	esteso	to extend	extension
intendere	inteso	to understand	to intend (UC)
pretendere	preteso	to claim	to pretend (UC), pretext
protendere	proteso	to stetch out	(none)
stendere	steso	to hang (clothes)	extend
sottintendere	sottinteso	to understand a hint	(none)
sopraintendere	soprainteso	to supervise	superintendent

Quiz on Rule 1

You know how to take this quiz: Fill in the blanks and check your answers against the next page. Where you are not sure, make an Educated Guess!

Italian Infinitive	Italian Past Participle	English Infinitive	Related English Word
offendere	_____	_____	_____
sospendere	_____	_____	_____
riprendere	_____	_____	_____
distendere	_____	_____	_____
scendere	_____	_____	_____
_____	steso	_____	_____
_____	appeso	_____	_____
_____	compreso	_____	_____
_____	conteso	_____	_____
_____	soprainteso	_____	_____
_____	_____	to defend	_____
_____	_____	to undertake	_____
_____	_____	to claim	_____
_____	_____	to spend	_____
_____	_____	to take, seize	_____
_____	_____	_____	intend
_____	_____	_____	fend
_____	_____	_____	surprise
_____	_____	_____	incendiary
_____	_____	_____	apprehend

Answers to Quiz on Rule 1

Italian Infinitive	Italian Past Participle	English Infinitive	Related English Word
offendere	offeso	to offend	offense
sospendere	sospeso	to suspend	suspense
riprendere	ripreso	to resume	reprise
distendere	disteso	to distend	distention
scendere	sceso	to descend	descent
stendere	steso	to hang (clothes)	extend
appendere	appeso	to append	appendix
comprendere	compreso	to comprise	comprehension
contendere	conteso	to contend	contention
sopraintendere	soprainteso	to supervise	superintendent
difendere	difeso	to defend	defense
intraprendere	intrapreso	to undertake	enterprise
pretendere	preteso	to claim	pretend (UC), pretext
spendere	speso	to spend	expense
prendere	preso	to take, seize	prehensile
intendere	inteso	to understand	intend
fendere	fesso	to fend off	fend
sorprendere	sorpreso	to surprise	surprise
accendere	acceso	to light, kindle	incendiary
apprendere	appreso	to learn	apprehend (UC)

Rule 2, Revisited

Now let's do a similar routine for Rule 2. In Table 6.2, we will list a number of verbs to which Rule 2 applies. Again, family members are grouped together; "orphans" are separated by spaces.

One important thing to note is that there is a significant minority of verbs ending in **-gere** or **-ggere** that do not go to the expected **-to** or **-tto**, but rather to **-so** or **-sso**; we will list them separately at the end of Table 6.2.

The verbs chosen for the table are among the most frequently used. Less frequently used verbs of this group will be discussed in Chapter 10. Now we restate Rule 2:

> <u>This is Rule 2</u>: Verbs ending in **-gere** or
> **-ggere** drop the ending and usually have it
> replaced by **-to** and **-tto**, respectively,
> e.g. fin/**gere** - fin/**to**; le/**ggere** - le/**tto**.
> For a few verbs, the participle ends in **-so**
> or **-sso**, e.g. **prefiggere** - **prefisso**.

TABLE 6.2: PARTICIPLES OF INFINITVES ENDING IN "-GERE" AND "-GGERE"

Italian Infinitive	Italian Past Participle	English Infinitive	Related English Word
affligere	afflitto	to afflict	affliction
infliggere	inflitto	to inflict	infliction
cingere	cinto	to cinch, gird	cinch
dipingere	dipinto	to depict, paint	depicted
distruggere	distrutto	to destroy	destruction
fingere	finto	to feign, pretend	feint
friggere	fritto	to fry	fries (QC)
fungere (da)	funto	to function (as)	functionary, defunct
giungere	giunto	to arrive	junction
aggiungere	aggiunto	to add	adjoining
congiungere	congiunto	to conjoin	conjoint
disgiungere	disgiunto	to unjoin	disjointed
ingiungere	ingiunto	to enjoin	injunction
raggiungere	raggiunto	to reach	(none)
soggiungere	soggiunto	to add verbally	subjoinder
sopraggiungere	sopraggiunto	to arrive unexpectedly	(none)
leggere	letto	to read	legible, lecture
sorgere	sorto	to rise	surge
risorgere	risorto	to rise again	resurgence, resurrection
spingere	spinto	to push	(none)
respingere	respinto	to reject	(none)

TABLE 6.2 (continued)

Italian Infinitive	Italian Past Participle	English Infinitive	Related English Word
volgere	volto	to turn	revolve (QC)
avvolgere	avvolto	to wrap around	(none)
capovolgere	capovolto	to turn upside down	(none)
coinvolgere	coinvolto	to involve together	involve (QC)
involgere	involto	to wrap up	involve (UC)
rivolger(si)	rivolto	to direct toward, address	revolve (UC)
sconvolgere	sconvolto	to confuse seriously	(none)
stravolgere	stravolto	to confuse meanings	(none)
svolgere	svolto	to carry out, take to a point	(none)
svolger(si)	svoltosi	to take place	(none)
travolgere	travolto	to sweep away	(none)

Major Exceptions: Participles Ending in "-so" or "-sso"

Italian Infinitive	Italian Past Participle	English Infinitive	Related English Word
affiggere	affisso	to affix	affix
crocifiggere	crocifisso	to crucify	crucifixion
prefiggere	prefisso	to prefix, fix beforehand	prefix
aspergere	asperso	to sprinkle	aspersion (UC)
emergere	emerso	to emerge	emergence
immergere	immerso	to immerse	immersion
sommergere	sommerso	to submerge	submersion
rifulgere	rifulso	to shine	refulgent
spargere	sparso	to scatter	sparse
tergere	terso	to wipe	terse (UC)
detergere	deterso	to cleanse	detergent

Quiz on Rule 2

Take the quiz in the usual way. Where you are not sure, Guess!

Italian Infinitive	Italian Past Participle	English Infinitive	Related English Word
friggere	_____	_____	_____
disgiungere	_____	_____	_____
leggere	_____	_____	_____
distruggere	_____	_____	_____
involgere	_____	_____	_____
_____	affisso	_____	_____
_____	immerso	_____	_____
_____	deterso	_____	_____
_____	funto	_____	_____
_____	aggiunto	_____	_____
_____	_____	to turn	_____
_____	_____	to confuse seriously	_____
_____	_____	to sprinkle	_____
_____	_____	to wipe	_____
_____	_____	to join, arrive	_____
_____	_____	_____	afflict(ion)
_____	_____	_____	conjoint
_____	_____	_____	surge
_____	_____	_____	cinch
_____	_____	_____	feint

Italian Infinitive	Italian Past Participle	English Infinitive	Related English Word
friggere	fritto	to fry	fried (QC)
disgiungere	disgiunto	to unjoin	disjointed
leggere	letto	to read	legible
distruggere	distrutto	to destroy	destruction
involgere	involto	to wrap up	involve (UC)
affiggere	affisso	to affix	affix
immergere	immerso	to immerse	immersion
detergere	deterso	to cleanse	detergent
fungere (da)	funto	to function (as)	functionary
aggiungere	aggiunto	to add	adjoining
volgere	volto	to turn	revolve (QC)
sconvolgere	sconvolto	to confuse seriously	(none)
aspergere	asperso	to sprinkle	aspersion (UC)
tergere	terso	to wipe	terse (UC)
giungere	giunto	to join, arrive	join
affliggere	afflitto	to afflict	afflict(ion)
congiungere	congiunto	to unite, conjoin	conjoint
sorgere	sorto	to rise, surge	surge
cingere	cinto	to cinch, gird	cinch
fingere	finto	to feign, pretend	feint

SEVEN.

POPULAR ITALIAN WORDS AND PHRASES

In this chapter you will find a number of words and phrases used by literate Italians in everyday speech and writing. Though not regularly included in language texts, the phrases pop up often and conspicuously enough in reading and conversation that they are worth learning. Make an effort to use them with your Italian-speaking friends, and you may be complimented on your intimacy with this portion of the language. First the words and phrases will be listed in alphabetical order in Italian (which is the way you will mostly likely encounter them), and then there will be a do-it-yourself quiz.

THE WORDS AND PHRASES

Key Word or Phrase	Example
1. **a posto**	Il benzinaio dice che l'acqua e l'olio sono **a posto**.
O.K.; in good order (lit., in place)	The gas station attendant says the the water and oil are <u>O.K.</u>
2. **andare bene (male)**	L'anno scorso, tutto **andava bene**.
to go well (poorly)	Last year, all <u>went well</u>.

3. **basta così**

   that's enough

   "No, grazie, **basta così.**

   "No, thank you, <u>that's enough.</u>"

4. **ci vuole, vogliono**

   it takes

   (Equivalent to the impersonal English construction of "How long <u>does it take</u> to get there?" or "How many hours <u>does it take</u> to get there?" Note, however, that although the verbs are always in the singular in English, in Italian, when the object is plural, so is the verb, as in these examples.)

   a. **Ci vuole** un'ora per finire l'esame.

      <u>It takes one</u> hour to finish the exam.

   b. **Ci vogliono** tre ore per finire l'esame.

      <u>It takes three</u> hours to finish the exam.

5. **come mai?!**

   how come?!; how could this ever be?!

   E' polacco il Papa? **Come mai?!**

   Is the Pope Polish? <u>How could this ever be</u>?!

6. **grosso modo**

   by and large

   Grosso modo, gli Americani sono più alti degli Italiani.

   <u>By and large,</u> the Americans are taller than the Italians.

7. **in genere**

   in general

   In genere, il clima in Liguria è mite.

   <u>In general,</u> the climate in Liguria is mild.

8. **magari**

   if only!; would that it were (often said in rueful tone)

   Magari, se lui avesse più tempo!

   <u>If only</u> he had more time!

9. **mica**

   at all;

   Non l'ho **mica** capito.

   I didn't understand it <u>at all</u>.

   or (somewhat dif-
   ferent meaning)
   perchance

   Non hai **mica** visto Susanna?

   You haven't <u>perchance</u> (<u>by any chance</u>)
   seen Susan?

10. **mica male**

    not bad (often in
    grudging approval or
    admiration)

    "Guarda quella donna," dice un ragazzo.
    "Mica male," dice l'altro.

    "Look at that woman," says one boy.
    "<u>Not bad</u>," says the other.

11. **non c'è male**

    not bad (a semi-
    superstitious way of
    avoiding saying things
    are clearly going well
    or poorly)

    "Come stai oggi?" **"Non c'è male."**

    "How are you today?" "<u>Not bad</u>."

12. **paragonare**

    to compare (related
    to <u>paragon</u>)

    Quando si **paragona** lui con lei ...

    When you <u>compare</u> him with her ...

13. **per quanto riguarda**

    regarding, in regard
    to; concerning

    Per quanto riguarda la statua ...

    <u>Concerning</u> the statue ...

14. **precisare**

    to specify,
    be precise

    "Vorrei un vino di Orvieto,"
    ho precisato.

    "I would like a wine from Orvieto,"
    I <u>specified</u>.

15. **può darsi**
    (+ subjunctive)

    maybe (lit., it
    can be given; often
    said with a shrug)

    Può darsi che mio fratello
    sia arrivato. Ma chissà?

    <u>Maybe</u> my brother has arrived.
    But who knows?

16. **rendersi conto**

    to realize
    (mentally)

    Finalmente **mi sono reso conto** che
    l'idea era falsa.

    Finally I <u>realized</u> that the idea was
    false.

17. **riuscire a**

Lui non **è** mai **riuscito a**
svegliarsi la mattina.

to manage to,
to succeed at

He never <u>managed to</u> wake up in the
morning.

18. **secondo ...**

Secondo Einstein, il tempo è la
quarta dimensione.

according to ...

<u>According to Einstein</u>, time is the
fourth dimension.

19. **sottolineare**

Ha sottolineato che i problemi non
sono semplici da superare.

to emphasize (lit.,
to underline)

<u>He emphasized</u> that the problems are not
easy to overcome.

20. **vale la pena**

Non **vale la pena** di arrabbiarsi con lei.

to be worth it;
to be worth the
trouble

It's not <u>worth it</u> to get mad at her.

QUIZ ON POPULAR WORDS AND PHRASES

Once you feel familiar with the words and phrases, take this quiz. For each item, make up a sentence using the Italian word or phrase, then translate it into English. There are two ways of evaluating your work: (1) If you have an Italian-speaking person around, have that person check your answers. (2) In the absence of such a person, compare your sentences against the examples given earlier.

1. Precisare. (Italian) _____

   (English) _____

2. Ci vuole, vogliono. _____

   _____

3. Magari! _____

   _____

4. Rendersi conto. _____

   _____

5. Come mai?! _____

   _____

6. Per quanto riguarda. _____

   _____

7. Basta così. _____

   _____

8. Può darsi. _____

   _____

9. In genere. _____

   _____

10. Sottolineare. _____

    _____

11. Paragonare. _____

_____

12. Mica male. _____

_____

13. Mica. _____

_____

14. Riuscire a. _____

_____

15. A posto. _____

_____

16. Grosso modo. _____

_____

17. Secondo lui. _____

_____

18. Andare bene (male). _____

_____

19. Non c'è male. _____

_____

20. Vale la pena. _____

_____

EIGHT.

UNFAITHFUL
COGNATES

TROUBLE AHEAD

As we warned you in an earlier chapter, there are words in the two languages that resemble each other in spelling and pronunciation but <u>differ markedly in meaning</u>, such as **pretendere** (to claim, make a claim on) and <u>to pretend</u> (to play-act).* We are calling such pairs <u>Unfaithful Cognates</u>.

The advertised advantages of making Educated Guesses are doubly offset when dealing with Unfaithful Cognates. Instead of avoiding memorization, two types of it will be needed! Be forewarned. To master this list, you will have to learn what the word really <u>does</u> mean, and also what it does <u>not</u> mean, even though it looks like something familiar. For example, **pretendere** <u>does</u> mean to have a claim on; it only rarely means to play-act.

---

* It wasn't until learning the meaning of **pretendere** in Italian that I corrected my childhood notion that a "pretender to a throne" was someone who had always <u>wanted</u>, without justification, to be a king or a queen and had therefore invented a plausible story and played a convincing role to advance his or her case.

If you are not in a mood to memorize now, just go over the list to sensitize yourself to the words so that if you see one in the future, you can say to yourself, "This is one of those strange ones; I better look it up before assuming I know what it means." You can also skip the quiz in this section until you want to do the memorization.

THE UNFAITHFUL COGNATES

The **Tendere** Family

The word **pretendere** is not the only Unfaithful Cognate in this family. Here are some others.

attendere
To await, expect, or to attend to tasks, but only rarely to attend (frequent) a school or church (which is **frequentare**) and <u>not</u> to pay attention (which is **fare attenzione a**).

contendere
To contend for a prize or a race, to be in contention, but <u>not</u> to have a point of view, e.g. <u>not</u> "I contend that ..." (which is **sostenere** or **ritenere**).

intendere
To understand (can be used as a synonym for **capire**), to mean or to signify, but only occasionally used to show intention in the sense of "I intend to go to Europe next year" (which is **avere intenzione di**).

stendere
To hang or extend, such as clothes on a line, but <u>never</u> to hang people (which is **impiccare** in Italian and inhumane in any language).

Other Unfaithful Cognates

There are other Unfaithful Cognates, some of which are verbs, some of which are not. Here they are.

affrontare
To face, confront, <u>not</u> to give offense, though the noun **l'affronto** means the same as <u>affront</u> in English.

annoiarsi
To be bored, <u>not</u> annoyed (which is **essere seccato**).

argomento
Argument in the sense of a discussion, as "the threads of the argument," <u>not</u> in the sense of a verbal brawl (which is **litigio**).

attuale	Present, currently, now. It is <u>not</u> used in the sense of "his <u>actual</u> worth" (which would be **il suo valore <u>effettivo</u>**).
bravo	clever, good, as in **bravo ragazzo**, a good boy, <u>not</u> brave, courageous (which is **coraggioso**).
deludere (p.p. deluso)	To disappoint, <u>not</u> to delude, lead astray (which is **ingannare**).
infastidire dare fastidio	To bother, be bothersome, <u>not</u> to be fastidious in the sense of being meticulous (though the word **fastidioso** exists in the latter sense).
ignorare	To be ignorant of, as well as to deliberately not pay attention to (this latter also being **far finta di non vedere**).
incidente	Accident, such as car accident, as well as <u>incident</u>.
libreria	Bookstore or bookshelf, <u>not</u> library (which is **biblioteca**).
occorrere	To be necessary, e.g. Per viaggiare **occore** denaro. (To travel, money <u>is necessary</u>.) Does <u>not</u> mean to occur, happen (which is **succedere**, **capitare**, or **accadere**).
parenti	Relatives, <u>not</u> parents (who are **genitori**).
rapire*	To kidnap, <u>not</u> to rape (which is **violentare**).

---

    * Italian newspapers, just like those in America, delight in stories involving sex, violence, and theft. To sort out such matters, examine this listing, which has several Unfaithful Cognates.

il rapimento	the abduction
la rapina	the robbery
rapinare	to rob
rapire	to abduct, kidnap
il rapitore	the abductor, kidnapper
il ratto	the rape, abduction
rubare	to steal
violentare	to rape
la violenza carnale	the rape

realizzare	To make something real, e.g. "He <u>realized</u> a large profit on his investment," <u>not</u> to understand, as in "He finally realized what I was saying" (which is **rendersi conto**).
riunione	Meeting, gathering, <u>not</u> reunion in the sense of a college reunion (which is **raduno**).
succedere	To happen or occur, or to succeed to a throne, <u>not</u> to be successful (which is the very common **riuscire**; also **avere successo**).

QUIZ ON UNFAITHFUL COGNATES

Translate the sentences in the spaces provided; check your work against the answers that follow. The underlined words come from the list just presented; translating them correctly is the most important part of this exercise.

1. He presented an interesting <u>argument</u>.

   _____

2. They had an awful <u>argument</u>.

   _____

3. You can find the book at the <u>library</u>.

   _____

4. You can buy the book at the <u>bookstore</u>.

   _____

5. <u>To attend</u> school, you must buy books.

   _____

6. You must <u>pay attention</u> to things.

   _____

7. I <u>am waiting</u> for Gennaro.

   _____

8. I _contend_ that the economy is improving.

RITENGO

9. _Intendo_ che cosa lui dice.

_____

10. _Ho intenzione_ di andare a teatro.

_____

11. _Abbiamo affrontato_ un momento difficile.

_____

12. _L'affronto_ mi ha fatto diventare triste.

_____

13. Ho incontrato _i parenti_ di Elena.

_____

14. Lui è un uomo che _mi dà fastidio_.

_____

15. C'è stato _un incidente_ grave sull'autostrada.

_____

16. Il discorso del presidente mi ha _deluso_.

_____

17. Per imparare, _occorre_ studiare.

_____

18. Cosa _succede_?

_____

19. La festa è stata un gran _successo_.

_____

20. Mi _sono reso conto_ che lui era un _bravo_ studente.

_____

1. He presented an interesting <u>argument</u>.
   Lui ha presentato un **argomento** interessante.

2. They had an awful <u>argument</u>.
   Hanno avuto un **litigio** terribile.

3. You can find the book at the <u>library</u>.
   Puoi trovare il libro alla **biblioteca**.

4. You can buy the book at the <u>bookstore</u>.
   Puoi comprare il libro alla **libreria**.

5. <u>To attend</u> school, you must buy books.
   Per **frequentare** la scuola, si devono comprare i libri.

6. You must <u>pay attention</u> to things.
   Devi **fare attenzione alle** cose.

7. I <u>am waiting</u> for Gennaro.
   Attendo (aspetto) Gennaro.

8. I <u>contend</u> that the economy is improving.
   Sostengo (ritengo) che l'economia migliori.

9. **Intendo** che cosa lui dice.
   <u>I understand</u> what he is saying.

10. **Ho intenzione** di andare a teatro.
    <u>I intend to</u> (<u>have the intention to</u>) go to the theatre.

11. **Abbiamo affrontato** un momento difficile.
    We <u>faced</u> (<u>confronted</u>) a difficult moment.

12. **L'affronto** mi ha fatto diventare triste.
    <u>The affront</u> made me become sad.

13. Ho incontrato **i parenti** di Elena.
    I met <u>the relatives</u> of Elena.

14. Lui è un uomo che **mi dà fastidio**.
    He is a man who <u>annoys</u> (<u>bothers</u>) me.

15. C'è stato **un incidente** grave sull'autostrada.
    There was a serious <u>accident</u> on the highway.

16. Il discorso del presidente mi ha **deluso**.
    The president's address <u>disappointed</u> me.

17. Per imparare, **occorre** studiare.
    In order to learn, <u>it is necessary</u> to study.

18. Cosa **succede**?
    <u>What's happening?</u> <u>What's going on?</u>

19. La festa è stata un gran **successo**.
    The party was a great <u>success</u>.

20. **Mi sono reso conto** che lui era un **bravo studente**.
    I <u>realized</u> that he was a <u>clever</u> (<u>good</u>) student.

NINE.

MORE VERBS AND THEIR FAMILIES

Chapters whose titles start with "More" are continuations of previous chapters! In the earlier chapters, a topic was introduced and as many examples as could be assimilated at one sitting were given. But the topic was not exhausted. Instead, after some intervening chapters for a change of pace, we are returning to the previous topic in order to add more examples. In Italian, we would say, "Riprendiamo" -- "We take (it) up again."

Bene, a questo punto riprendiamo l'argomento dei verbi e delle loro famiglie che abbiamo visto per la prima volta nel Chapter 5, "Verbs and Their Families: A First Approximation." In it we saw that irregularities in the present tense and the formation of the past participle usually were regular, that is, were shared by all members of a family. Note that irregularities in the present tense are reflected when forming the imperative and the subjunctive, both topics of later chapters. Keeping an eye out for such things as the intrusive "g" here will also pay off handsomely later.

We have selected eight more verb families to present. We will give the conjugation of the main verb in the present only if it is irregular, then list family members and then make a brief comment about features of the family.

The verb families we have chosen to present are the following: **cedere, crescere, dire, fare, scrivere, stare, togliere,** and **venire.**

THE VERBS AND THEIR FAMILIES

Cedere: To Cede, Yield, Give

These verbs are regular in the present tense.

Italian Infinitive	Italian Past Participle	English Infinitive	Related English Word
cedere	ceduto	to cede, give	cede
accedere	accesso	to approach, comply with	access, accede
antecedere	anteceduto	to precede	antecedent
concedere	concesso	to concede	concede
decedere	deceduto	to die	decedent
incedere	incesso	to walk	(none)
precedere	preceduto	to precede	precede
procedere	proceduto	to proceed	procession
recedere	receduto	to recede	recession
retrocedere	retrocesso	to degrade	retrocession, cede back
succedere	successo	to happen	succession

In this family, the corresponding English verbs follow the Italian infinitive; that is, they often end in -cede (-ceed). The corresponding English nouns, on the other hand, usually follow the Italian past participle, -cesso, e.g.: con**cedere** - con**cesso** and to con**cede** - con**cess**ion.

Some of these verbs are regular in the past participle, i.e., they end in -ceduto; others come close to following our fakeout rule and end in -cesso. Sorry about that.

Once again a reminder about **succedere**: Its primary meaning is to happen, or to succeed in the sense of a series of events, one succeeding another. It does not mean to succeed in a venture (which is **avere successo** or **riuscire**).

Crescere: To Grow, Swell

These verbs are regular in the present tense.

Italian Infinitive	Italian Past Participle	English Infinitive	Related English Word
crescere	cresciuto	to increase, grow	crescendo
accrescere	accresciuto	to increase	accretion
decrescere	decresciuto	to decrease	decrease
rincrescere	rincresciuto	to regret	(none)

The Italian infinitive, **crescere**, is related to the English -crease, e.g. **descrescere** - to <u>decrease</u>. The present participle of **crescere** is **crescendo**, which should mean "a growing, a swelling." Contemporary usage, borrowed mistakenly from music and applied by extension to other aspects of English, treats **crescendo** as if it means to reach a peak or climax, e.g. "At the final touchdown, the crowd's excitement reached a **crescendo**." We plead with the purists among you to preserve the proper meaning, e.g. "The crowd experienced a **crescendo** (growing, swelling) of excitement," knowing full well that the purists in this world are doomed to virtuous disappointment.

Dire: To Say, Tell

dico diciamo
dici dite
dice dicono

Italian Infinitive	Italian Past Participle	English Infinitive	Related English Word
dire	detto	to say, tell	dictum, diction
benedire	benedetto	to bless	benediction
contraddire	contraddetto	to contradict	contradiction
disdire	disdetto	to unsay, retract	(none)
interdire	interdetto	to interdict, forbid	interdiction
maledire	maledetto	to curse	malediction
predire	predetto	to predict	prediction
ridire	ridetto	to repeat, find fault with	(none)

This is a nice family; there are lots of Italian/English correspondences, so they should be easy to learn. And, as inspection quickly reveals, **-detto**, the Italian past participle, usually corresponds to the English <u>-dict</u> (verb) or <u>-diction</u> (noun), e.g.:

contraddire   contraddetto   to contra<u>dict</u>   contra<u>diction</u>

Fare: To Make, Do

faccio facciamo
fai fate
fa fanno

Italian Infinitive	Italian Past Participle	English Infinitive	Related English Word
fare	fatto	to make, do	factotum (QC)
assuefare(si)	assuefatto	to accustom, get used to	(none)
contraffare	contraffatto	to counterfeit	counterfeit (QC)
disfare	disfatto	to unmake, undo	(none)
rifare	rifatto	to make again	refectory (QC)
sfare	sfatto	to undo	(none)
soddisfare	soddisfatto	to satisfy	satisfaction
sopraffare	sopraffatto	to overwhelm	(none)
stupefare	stupefatto	to stupefy	stupefaction
torrefare	torrefatto	to roast (e.g., coffee beans)	(none)
tumefare	tumefatto	to tumefy, cause to swell	tumefaction

Note that the Italian past participle, **-fatto**, can correspond to the English -fy for a verb and -fact(ion) for a noun, e.g.:

soddis**fare**	soddis**fatto**	satis<u>fy</u>	satis<u>faction</u>

Scrivere: To Write

This family is regular in the present tense.

Italian Infinitive	Italian Past Participle	English Infinitive	Related English Word
scrivere	scritto	to write	scribe, script
ascrivere	ascritto	to ascribe	ascription
descrivere	descritto	to describe	description
iscrivere	iscritto	to inscribe, enroll	inscription
prescrivere	prescritto	to prescribe	prescription
proscrivere	proscritto	to proscribe	proscription
riscrivere	riscritto	to write again	(none)
sottoscrivere	sottoscritto	to subscribe, underwrite	subscription (poss. UC)
trascrivere	trascritto	to transcribe	transcription

Here's a lovely family to contemplate. The root verb and its eight family members nearly all have related English verbs and nouns, and the transformations are quite regular, so you can translate backwards, from English into Italian, in nearly every case, with the English verb ending in -scribe and the English noun in -scription.

The word **iscrivere**, in addition to "inscribe," also means "to enroll," e.g. "Ci sono 80 studenti **iscritti** nella scuola" ("There are 80 students <u>enrolled</u> in the school"). One uses **sottoscrivere** (<u>to subscribe</u>) in the sense of subscribing to a bond issue or to assent to a proposal; it does <u>not</u> mean to subscribe to a magazine, which is **abbonarsi**.

Stare: To Stay, Be, Remain, Stand

sto	stiamo
stai	state
sta	stanno

Italian Infinitive	Italian Past Participle	English Infinitive	Related English Word
stare	stato	to be, stay	state
constatare	constatato	to ascertain	(none)
contrastare	contrastato	to contrast	contrast
costare	costato	to cost	cost
prestare	prestato	to lend	(none)
restare	restato	to remain	rest
sostare	sostato	to stop, pause	(none)
sottostare	sottostato	to be below	substance
sovrastare	sovrastato	to dominate	(none)

Three derivatives of this family deserve note. The noun from **sostare** (to stop, pause) is **la sosta**; and in potential parking places all over Italy, there are signs reading "Vietata **la sosta**" or "Divieto di **Sosta**": <u>Parking</u> Prohibited.

A second derivative is from **restare** (<u>to remain</u>); the noun is **il resto**, and that often means the change you get back after paying for something: "Ecco, **il resto**"; "Here is the <u>change</u>."

A third derivative is from **prestare** (<u>to lend</u>). A common idiom is **prendere in prestito**, meaning <u>to take as a loan</u>.

Finally, here is a very common and useful idiom: **stare per** means <u>to be on the verge of</u>; <u>to be about to</u>. "**Sto per** andare fuori"; "<u>I'm just about to</u> go out."

Togliere: To Take Away, Remove

tolgo	togliamo
togli	togliete
toglie	tolgono

Togliere is one of several verbs that end in **-gliere** in the infinitive and **-olto** in the past participle (**tolto**). Some of the family members are more cousins than siblings, but they all carry a weird gene for the intrusive "g," in that the **-lg-** of the first person singular and third person plural reverses itself and becomes **-gl-** in the other forms, as seen above.

Italian Infinitive	Italian Past Participle	English Infinitive	Related English Word
togliere	tolto	to take away	(none)
cogliere	colto	to collect	collect (QC)
accogliere	accolto	to greet, welcome	(none)
raccogliere	raccolto	to pick up again	(none)
scegliere	scelto	to select, choose	select (QC)
sciogliere	sciolto	to dissolve	dissolve (QC)

Some of these verbs, too, are Quasi-Cognates with English, as in this list:

> **cogliere** - to <u>collect</u>
> **scegliere** - to <u>select</u>
> **sciogliere** - to <u>dissolve</u>

The verb **raccogliere** means <u>to pick up, gather again</u> and is an Unfaithful Cognate of <u>recollect</u> (used in English in the sense of "to remember").

Togliersi la vita is a frequent way newspapers refer to suicides: "Lui **si è tolto** la vita"; "He <u>took away</u> his life."

Venire: To Come

vengo   veniamo
vieni   venite
viene   vengono

Italian Infinitive	Italian Past Participle	English Infinitive	Related English Word
venire	venuto	to come	(none)
avvenire	avvenuto	to happen, occur	(none)
contravvenire	contravvenuto	to contravene	contravention
convenire	convenuto	to convene	convent, -tion
divenire	divenuto	to become	(none)

intervenire	intervenuto	to intervene	intervention
prevenire	prevenuto	to forewarn	prevention
provenire	provenuto	to come (from)	provenance
rinvenire	rinvenuto	to come up	(none)
sopravvenire	sopravvenuto	to supervene, turn up	supervene

sovvenire	sovvenuto	to remember	souvenir
svenire	svenuto	to faint	(none)

Please note that many of the corresponding English verbs in this family end in -vene or -vent, and that the nouns often end in -vention, e.g.:

con**venire**	con**venuto**	to con<u>vene</u>	con<u>vention</u>

Please also note that the verb **divenire** (<u>to become</u>) is a synonym for the more familiar **diventare**.

QUIZ ON MORE VERB FAMILIES

    This quiz is like many others you have taken. Fill in the three blanks on each line; check the next page for the answers. Where you are not sure, make an Educated Guess!

Italian Infinitive	Italian Past Participle	English Infinitive	Related English Word
scegliere	_____	_____	_____
costare	_____	_____	_____
prevenire	_____	_____	_____
malfare	_____	_____	_____
descrivere	_____	_____	_____
_____	recesso	_____	_____
_____	descreciuto	_____	_____
_____	contraddetto	_____	_____
_____	soddisfatto	_____	_____
_____	contrastato	_____	_____
_____	_____	to comply with, approach	_____
_____	_____	to dissolve	_____
_____	_____	to become	_____
_____	_____	to bless	_____
_____	_____	to happen, succeed	_____
_____	_____	_____	stupefaction
_____	_____	_____	collect (QC)
_____	_____	_____	rest, remainder
_____	_____	_____	supervene
_____	_____	_____	concession

Answers to Quiz on More Verb Families

Italian Infinitive	Italian Past Participle	English Infinitive	Related English Word
scegliere	scelto	to select, choose	select (QC)
costare	costato	to cost	cost
prevenire	prevenuto	to prevent	prevention
malfare	malfatto	to misbehave	malefactor
descrivere	descritto	to describe	description
recedere	recesso	to recede	recession
decrescere	descreciuto	to decrease	decrease
contraddire	contraddetto	to contradict	contradiction
soddisfare	soddisfatto	to satisfy	satisfaction
contrastare	contrastato	to contrast	contrast
accedere	accesso	to comply with, approach	access; accede
sciogliere	sciolto	to dissolve	dissolve (QC)
divenire	divenuto	to become	(none)
benedire	benedetto	to bless	benediction
succedere	successo	to happen, succeed	succession
stupefare	stupefatto	to stupefy	stupefaction
cogliere	colto	to collect	collect (QC)
restare	restato	to remain	rest, remainder
sopravvenire	sopravvenuto	to supervene	supervene
concedere	concesso	to concede	concession

TEN

MORE VERBS WHOSE PAST PARTICIPLES CAN BE FAKED OUT

In the earlier chapter, "Faking Out Irregular Past Participles," you were provided with two rules. Rule 1 dealt with verbs whose infinitives ended in **-dere** and **-ndere**, and it stated that for the participle, the ending of the infinitive was replaced by **-so**, e.g.:

acce/**ndere**	acce/**so**
spe/**ndere**	spe/**so**
ucci/**dere**	ucci/**so**

Rule 2 dealt with verbs ending in **-gere** and **-ggere** and stated that the participles ended usually with **-to** and **-tto**, respectively, though sometimes they ended with **-so** and **-sso**, e.g.:

fin/**gere**	fin/**to**
fri/**ggere**	fri/**tto**
emer/**gere**	emer/**so**
prefi/**ggere**	prefi/**sso**

Soon we will show more examples that follow these rules. Knowing these past participles will take on additional importance when we get to the chapter "How to Recognize, Remember, and Even Make, Nouns from Verbs." You will see that many, many nouns are more closely related to participles than infinitives, so by knowing how to fake out the participle, you will enhance considerably your ability to make Educated Guesses about nouns.

VERBS ENDING IN "-DERE"

When we presented Rule 1 in our earlier chapter, we listed only verbs whose infinitives ended in **-ndere**, and we left for now those ending in **-adere**, **-edere**, **-idere**, **-ondere**, and **-udere**.

The most important of them are listed below. Family members are grouped together. Look them over and then take the quiz that follows.

Italian Infinitive	Italian Past Participle	English Infinitive	Related English Word
ardere	arso	to burn	arson, ardent
chiedere	chiesto*	to ask	quest
chiudere	chiuso	to close	closure
concludere	concluso	to conclude	conclusion
accludere	accluso	to enclose	enclosed
escludere	escluso	to exclude	exclusive
includere	incluso	to include	inclusive
decidere	deciso	to decide	decisive
coincidere	coinciso	to coincide	coincidence
incidere	inciso	to incise	incisive
uccidere	ucciso	to kill	homicide (QC)
deludere	deluso	to disappoint	delusion (UC)
eludere	eluso	to elude	elusive
illudere	illuso	to deceive	illusion
dividere	diviso	to divide	division
condividere	condiviso	to share	(none)
evadere	evaso	to evade	evasion
invadere	invaso	to invade	invasion
pervadere	pervaso	to pervade	pervasive
fondere	fuso	to fuse, melt	fusion
confondere	confuso	to confuse	confusion
diffondere	diffuso	to diffuse, spread	diffusion
infondere	infuso	to infuse	infusion
trasfondere	trasfuso	to transfuse	transfusion

_____

* Slight variant to the **-so** rule.

Italian Infinitive	Italian Past Participle	English Infinitive	Related English Word
mordere	morso	to bite	mordant, morsel
nascondere	nascosto*	to hide	(none)
perdere	perso, perduto	to lose	perdition
persuadere	persuaso	to persuade	persuasive, persuasion
radere	raso	to shave	razor, raze (UC)
ridere	riso	to laugh	risible
rispondere	risposto *	to respond	response
succedere	successo	to happen, succeed	succession
vedere	visto *, veduto	to see, view	vision; vista
prevedere	previsto *	to forecast	preview
provvedere	provvisto *	to provide	provision

* Slight variant to the **-so** rule.

Here is another quiz, with three blanks on each line for you to fill in. As usual, when you are not sure, make an Educated Guess!

Italian Infinitive	Italian Past Participle	English Infinitive	Related English Word
confondere	_____	_____	_____
rispondere	_____	_____	_____
escludere	_____	_____	_____
uccidere	_____	_____	_____
persuadere	_____	_____	_____
_____	perso, perduto	_____	_____
_____	provvisto	_____	_____
_____	infuso	_____	_____
_____	deluso	_____	_____
_____	incluso	_____	_____
_____	_____	to divide	_____
_____	_____	to burn	_____
_____	_____	to see	_____
_____	_____	to diffuse, spread	_____
_____	_____	_____	conclusion
_____	_____	_____	closure
_____	_____	_____	risibility
_____	_____	_____	mordant, morsel

Answers to Quiz on More Verbs Ending in "-dere"

Italian Infinitive	Italian Past Participle	English Infinitive	Related English Word
confondere	confuso	to confuse	confusion
rispondere	risposto	to respond	response
escludere	escluso	to exclude	exclusive
uccidere	ucciso	to kill	homicide (QC)
persuadere	persuaso	to persuade	persuasive, persuasion
perdere	perso, perduto	to lose	perdition
provvedere	provvisto	to provide	provision
infondere	infuso	to infuse	infusion
deludere	deluso	to disappoint	delusion (UC)
includere	incluso	to include	inclusion
dividere	diviso	to divide	division
ardere	arso	to burn	arson, ardent
vedere	visto	to see	vision, vista
diffondere	diffuso	to diffuse, spread	diffusion
concludere	concluso	to conclude	conclusion
chiudere	chiuso	to close	closure
ridere	riso	to laugh	risibility
mordere	morso	to bite	mordant, morsel

VERBS ENDING IN "-GERE" AND "-GGERE"

We are presenting here only the 20 most common verbs with these endings. For the participle, drop the **-gere** or **-ggere** and substitute **-to** or **-tto**. Family members are grouped together; "orphans" are separated. Because there are so few verbs, we won't bother with a quiz after this presentation.

Italian Infinitive	Italian Past Participle	English Infinitive	Related English Word
accorgersi	accorto	to perceive	(none)
correggere	corretto	to correct	correction
dipingere	dipinto	to paint, depict	depiction
dirigere	diretto	to direct, manage	director
erigere	eretto	to erect	erection
distruggere	distrutto	to destroy	destruction
eleggere	eletto	to elect	election
sconfiggere	sconfitto	to defeat, overturn	(none)
frangere	franto	to break	frangible, fraction
indulgere	indulto	to indulge	indulgence
piangere	pianto	to cry	plaintive
compiangere	compianto	to pity	complain (UC)
prediligere	prediletto	to prefer	predilection
proteggere	protetto	to protect	protection
sorgere	sorto	to rise	surge
insorgere	insorto	to rebel	insurrection
risorgere	risorto	to rise again	resurgence
stringere	stretto*	to squeeze	stricture
costringere	costretto*	to constrain	constraint
tingere	tinto	to dye, color	tint

* Slight variant to the **-to** rule.

ELEVEN.

HOW TO RECOGNIZE, REMEMBER, AND EVEN MAKE, NOUNS FROM VERBS

AMARE AMATO L'AMORE

Many Italian nouns are closely related to certain Italian verbs. There are regular patterns of transformation from verb form to noun, and you will have an opportunity to discover them for yourself, as you have in earlier chapters. Once you are aware of these patterns, it will be much easier to recognize and remember a noun deriving from a verb you already know. Often you will be able to guess correctly at the meaning of a noun you have never seen before!

There will be exceptions to the rules, of course, so again a note of caution should be injected against promiscuous application of them. Let them be an aid, not a master, for remembering and Educated Guessing.

The patterns for the first conjugation (e.g. **parlare**) are somewhat different from those of the second and third conjugations (e.g. **credere, dormire**). We will look at each of the conjugations soon, but first let's consider a rule that applies to all three.

A Rule Involving Infinitives

Inspect these examples and see if you can detect the relationship between the Italian verb and noun, and if you can detect how this particular usage corresponds to an equivalent English construction.

1. **Il dormire** fa bene a tutti.
   <u>Sleeping</u> (<u>to sleep</u>) is good for everybody.

2. **Il mangiare** dei cibi italiani è un piacere.
   <u>Eating</u> (<u>to eat</u>) Italian foods is a pleasure.

Relationship of Italian verb and noun: _____

Corresponding English construction: _____

These examples show this principle: The Italian infinitive may be used as a singular masculine noun (e.g. **il dormire**) when the English would use the present participle or, more rarely, the infinitive (e.g. <u>sleeping</u>, <u>to sleep</u>).

This is a respected Italian construction, not merely a shortcut used by foreigners. It should be used <u>only</u> when the English would call for a verb form (participle or infinitive). It should <u>not</u> be used when the English would clearly call for a noun. Thus, in "I had a good <u>sleep</u> last night," clearly this is a noun and the corresponding Italian noun, **la dormita**, would have to be used.

VERBS OF THE FIRST CONJUGATION

Verbs of the first conjugation appear more frequently than those of the second and third conjugations. Over two-thirds of first-conjugation verbs have related nouns, and the vast majority of these nouns follow one of the three patterns we are about to discover.

We will present the material for all three conjugations in these four columns: Italian infinitive, Italian past participle, Italian noun(s), English noun(s). The English nouns will be cognates whenever they exist.

Occasionally, there will be two or three Italian nouns deriving from the same verb. The first noun shown will be the one most important to demonstrate a point. Others will listed beneath it, with ditto marks under the infinitive and past participle to show that those nouns too are related to the same verb. See the examples on the next page.

Italian Infinitive	Italian Past Participle	Italian Noun	English Noun
fermare	fermato	il fermo	the lock, catch
"	"	la fermata	the stop, halt

A First Approximation

Group 1. Now to Group (and pattern) 1 of the first-conjugation verbs. Inspect the group and see if you can find a relationship pattern between the Italian noun and one of its two verb forms (infinitive, past participle) or their derivatives.

Italian Infinitive	Italian Past Participle	Italian Noun	English Noun
aiutare	aiutato	l'aiuto	the aid, help
gettare	gettato	il getto	the throw
ricordare	ricordato	il ricordo	the memory, souvenir
scontare	scontato	lo sconto	the discount
toccare	toccato	il tocco	the touch
usare	usato	l'uso	the use

   Pattern(s) I discern: _____

_____

Group 2. Now tackle this group, and be sure to include inspection of the English nouns as part of your musings.

Italian Infinitive	Italian Past Participle	Italian Noun	English Noun
manifestare	manifestato	la manifestazione	the manifestation
"	"	il manifesto	the manifesto, placard
pubblicare	pubblicato	la pubblicazione	the publication
rivelare	rivelato	la rivelazione	the revelation
salvare	salvato	la salvazione	the salvation
spiegare	spiegato	la spiegazione	the explanation
trattare	trattato	il trattamento	the treatment

   Pattern(s) I discern: _____

_____

<u>Group 3</u>. Here is Group 3; again, see if you can find a pattern.

Italian Infinitive	Italian Past Participle	Italian Noun	English Noun
andare	andato	l'andata	the going
chiamare	chiamato	la chiamata	the (phone) call
entrare	entrato	l'entrata	the entrance
fermare	fermato	la fermata	the stop, halt

Pattern(s) I discern: _____

_____

<u>Group 1 Pattern</u>. The pattern for Group 1 is that the Italian noun is the same as the first person singular of the verb. For example, for the verb **toccare**, its first person singular is **tocco** (<u>I touch</u>). The noun is **il tocco**, (<u>the touch</u>). If you look at the examples, for all of them, the Italian noun is the same as the first person singular, e.g. **aiuto - l'aiuto; ricordo - il ricordo**, etc.

The past participle does not figure in any of them. It is a red herring we threw in so that now you can throw it out.

About one third of all first-conjugation verbs have a related noun that conforms to this pattern.

<u>Group 2 Pattern</u>. The pattern for Group 2 is that there are parallel endings for the English and Italian nouns. Where an Italian noun ends in **-zione** or **-amento**, the English noun ends in <u>-tion</u> or <u>-ment</u>, as in spiega**zione** - explana<u>tion</u>; tratta**mento** - treat<u>ment</u>.

About one-quarter of all first-conjugation verbs have a related noun that conforms to this pattern.

<u>Group 3 Pattern</u>. The pattern for Group 3 is that of the Past Participle Feminized. That is, the noun is nothing more than the past participle in drag, e.g. entrare - **entrato** - **l'entrata** - the entrance. Here **entrato** has taken estrogens to become **l'entrata**. Frequently such a transformation takes place with an intransitive verb of motion (to go, enter, stop, etc.).

About one-fifth of all first-conjugation verbs have related nouns that conform to this pattern.

A Second Approximation

Table 11.1 shows 26 commonly used first-conjugation verbs and nouns. Three verbs fail to have <u>at least</u> one related noun that conforms to the rules just given. See if you can find those three as well as determine which patterns all the others follow.

TABLE 11.1. FIRST-CONJUGATION VERBS AND NOUNS

Italian Infinitive	Italian Past Participle	Italian Noun	English Noun
aiutare	aiutato	l'aiuto	the aid, help
andare	andato	l'andata	the going
"	"	l'andamento	the course
"	"	l'andatura	the walk, gait
assicurare	assicurato	l'assicurazione	the insurance
baciare	baciato	il bacio	the kiss
cambiare	cambiato	il cambio	the money
"	"	il cambiamento	the exchange
chiamare	chiamato	la chiamata	the call
cominciare	cominciato	il cominciamento*	the commencement, beginning
domandare	domandato	la domanda	the question
entrare	entrato	l'entrata	the entrance
fermare	fermato	il fermo	the lock, catch
"	"	la fermata	the stop, halt
formare	formato	la forma	the form
gettare	gettato	il getto	the throw
iniziare	iniziato	l'inizio	the start, initiation (QC)
manifestare	manifestato	il manifesto	the manifesto, placard
"	"	la manifestazione	the manifestation
regalare	regalato	il regàlo	the gift
regolare	regolato	la règola	the rule
"	"	il regolamento	the regulation
ricordare	ricordato	il ricordo	the memory, souvenir
ritornare	ritornato	il ritorno	the return
rivelare	rivelato	la rivelazione	the revelation
salutare	salutato	il saluto	the salutation, greeting
salvare	salvato	la salvazione	the salvation (relig.)
"	"	la salvezza	the salvation, escape
"	"	il salvataggio	the saving of a life
segnare	segnato	il segno	the signal, sign
spiegare	spiegato	la spiegazione	the explanation
toccare	toccato	il tocco	the touch
trattare	trattato	il trattamento	the treatment
usare	usato	l'uso	the use

---

* Archaic and very rarely used.

Did you find the <u>three verbs</u> in Table 11.1 that <u>did not</u> conform to one of the three patterns? They are: **domandare - la domanda; formare - la forma;** and **regolare - la règola** and **il regolamento.**

Shortly you will be given a quiz in which you will be provided with first-conjugation infinitives and asked to supply the past participle and the Italian and English nouns. How best to proceed?

1. Make sure you know the meaning of the infinitive. Look it up in a dictionary if you need to.

2. If there is a corresponding English noun that ends in <u>-tion</u> or <u>-ment</u>, there is probably a corresponding Italian noun ending in **-zione** or **-mento,** etc. Plug it in.

3. If the verb is an intransitive verb of motion, try the feminization of the past participle, e.g. **entrare - entrato - l'entrata -** <u>the entrance</u>.

4. Otherwise, the noun most likely is the same as the first-person singular of the verb, e.g. **toccare - toccato - il tocco -** <u>the touch</u>.

5. Sometime your ear, eye, or intuition tells you to go in a direction contrary to these rules. If so, follow that inner voice.

Quiz on First-Conjunction Verbs and Their Nouns

Italian Infinitive	Italian Past Participle	Italian Noun	English Noun
abbandonare	_____	_____	_____
alzarsi	_____	_____	_____
amare	_____	_____	_____
arrivare	_____	_____	_____
ascoltare	_____	_____	_____
camminare	_____	_____	_____
cercare	_____	_____	_____
continuare	_____	_____	_____
creare	_____	_____	_____
dimostrare	_____	_____	_____
evitare	_____	_____	_____
guardare	_____	_____	_____
incontrare	_____	_____	_____
mutare	_____	_____	_____
osservare	_____	_____	_____
passare	_____	_____	_____
restare	_____	_____	_____
scherzare	_____	_____	_____
studiare	_____	_____	_____
tentare	_____	_____	_____

Answers to Quiz on First-Conjugation Verbs and Their Nouns

Italian Infinitive	Italian Past Participle	Italian Noun	English Noun
abbandonare	abbandonato	l'abbandono	the abandonment
alzarsi	alzato	l'alzata	the rising up
amare	amato	l'amore	the love
arrivare	arrivato	l'arrivo	the arrival
ascoltare	ascoltato	l'ascolto	the listening
camminare	camminato	il cammino	the way
"	"	la camminata	the stroll
cercare	cercato	la cerca (rare)	the search (QC)
continuare	continuato	la continuazione	the continuation
creare	creato	il creato	the shape
"	"	la creazione	the creation
dimostrare	dimostrato	la dimostrazione	the demonstration
evitare	evitato	l'evitare	the avoidance
guardare	guardato	la guardata	the glance
incontrare	incontrato	l'incontro	the encounter (QC)
mutare	mutato	il mutamento	the change
"	"	la mutazione	the mutation
osservare	osservato	l'osservazione	the observation
passare	passato	il passo	the pass, step
"	"	il passaggio	the passage of time
restare	restato	il resto	the change, remainder
scherzare	scherzato	lo scherzo	the joke
studiare	studiato	lo studio	the study
tentare	tentato	il tentativo	the attempt (QC)

VERBS OF THE SECOND CONJUGATION

A First Approximation

Things are a bit different with the second conjugation, as you will see with our old friends, the **mettere** family, presented below. Look at it and see what patterns you can discern; there are at least three. As before, look at the Italian noun and then compare it to its infinitive and its past participle. Jot down your thoughts in the spaces provided.

Italian Infinitive	Italian Past Participle	Italian Noun	English Noun
mettere	messo	La Messa	the Mass (relig.)
ammettere	ammesso	l'ammissione	the admission
commettere	commesso	il, la commesso(a)	the clerk
		la commissione	the commission

compromettere	compromesso	il compromesso	the compromise
dimetter(si)	dimesso	la dimissione	the dismissal, resignation
emettere	emesso	l'emissione	the emission
immettere	immesso	l'immissione	the letting in
intrometter(si)	intromesso	l'intromissione	the interference, intromission
omettere	omesso	l'omissione	the omission
permettere	permesso	il permesso	the permission
premettere	premesso	la premessa	the premise
promettere	promesso	la promessa	the promise
		il, la promesso(a)	the bethrothed
rimettere	rimesso	la remissione	the remission
		la rimessa	the remittance
ripromettere	ripromesso	(none)	(none)
scommettere	scommesso	la scommessa	the bet, wager
smettere	smesso	(none)	the cessation
sottometter(si)	sottomesso	la sottomissione	the submission, subjection
trasmettere	trasmesso	la trasmissione	the transmission

Patterns I discern: 1. _____

2. _____

3. _____

Patterns for the **Mettere** Family

1. The Past Participle Triumphant. In the extensive **mettere** family, <u>every</u> Italian noun is taken from the stem of the past participle rather than from the infinitive! Note that each participle ends in **-messo**, and that each Italian noun contains **-mess-** or **-miss-**, as shown in the examples below.

This persistence of the participle in the noun is true for about 95% of all nouns derived from second-conjugation verbs. Therefore, <u>the Past Participle Triumphant is very important!</u>

Italian Infinitive	Italian Past Participle	Italian Noun	English Noun
mettere	messo	La Messa	the Mass (relig.)
ammettere	ammesso	l'ammissione	the admission
commettere	commesso	il commesso(a)	the clerk
		la commissione	the commission
compromettere	compromesso	il compromesso	the compromise
dimetter(si)	dimesso	la dimissione	the dismissal, resignation
emettere	emesso	l'emissione	the emission

Many chapters ago, you learned how to fake out the irregular past participles for most verbs requiring it. Now you have an important key on how to make nouns out of them.

2. The Feminine Nearly Triumphant. All but four of the **mettere** nouns are feminine. As shown below, two are bisexual pairs and two are unambiguously masculine. This is true generally for the second conjugation: It's a woman's world where rarely is heard a masculine word.

Bisexual Pairs

commettere	commesso	il, la commesso(a)	the clerk
		la commissione	the commission
promettere	promesso	la promessa	the promise
		il, la promesso(a)	the betrothed

Unambiguous Masculines

compromettere	compromesso	il compromesso	the compromise
permettere	permesso	il permesso	the permission

Both clerks and betrothed can be male or female. Commissions and promises are only female.

Compromises and permissions are only male.

All other Italian nouns from the **mettere** family are only female.

3. Parallel Endings in English and Italian. Most of the corresponding English nouns from this family end in -sion and have an Italian counterpart ending in **-ssione**. Thus if you know the English noun, in most cases you can translate backward and arrive at the Italian. Below are examples that conform to this pattern, plus a few nonconformists.

Conformers

ammissione	admission
commissione	commission
emissione	emission
intromissione	intromission
omissione	omission
remissione	remission
sottomissione	submission
trasmissione	transmission

Exceptions

dimissione	resignation, dismissal
permesso	permission

Go back now to the middle of page 105 and see how close you came in your own words to finding these patterns for the **mettere** family:

1. The Past Participle Triumphant.

2. The Feminine Nearly Triumphant.

3. Parallel Endings in English and Italian.

These three patterns are quite prevalent throughout the second conjugation, so keep them in mind as we proceed.

A Second Approximation

A simple, useful truth struck me one cold winter's day as I was riding on the bus from Genova to Nervi and mulling over my grammar. I could barely believe how well it works, but it does! Try to discover it for yourself. In the listing below, see what patterns you can find between the Italian noun and one of its verb forms, and rejoice in the discovery.

Italian Infinitive	Italian Past Participle	Italian Noun	English Noun
attendere	atteso	l'attesa	the waiting
difendere	difeso	la difesa	the defense
discendere	disceso	la discesa	the descent
rendere	reso	la resa	the rendering, restitution
arrendere	arreso	l'arresa	the surrender
spendere	speso	la spesa	the expense

Patterns I discern: _____

_____

Now go to the next page and compare our discoveries.

The simple, useful truth is this:

> The noun is the feminization
> of the past participle!

Look at **attendere** (to wait). Its past participle is **atteso.** Change it to the feminine, and you have **l'attesa** (the waiting). Try **difendere** (to defend); the past participle is **difeso,** which, as a feminine noun, is **la difesa** (the defense).

It's that simple. Note that once again that both the Past Participle and the Feminine are Triumphant.

Surely these verbs look familiar to you. They are the ones ending in **-dere** and **-ndere** that we encountered when first learning how to fake out irregular past participles. When we move on, we will see that not too many of these verbs have English counterparts ending in <u>-sion</u>, <u>-tion</u>, <u>-ment</u>, and the like.

We must therefore slightly expand our simple, useful truth to the following:

> For verbs whose infinitive ends in
> **-dere** or **-ndere,** and for which
> there is no English noun ending in
> <u>-sion</u> and the like, the Italian
> noun is almost always the feminine
> of the past participle.

See the following list for examples.

Italian Infinitive	Italian Past Participle	Italian Noun	English Noun
attendere	atteso	l'attesa	the waiting
contendere	conteso	la contesa	the contest
distendere	disteso	la distesa	the expanse
intendere	inteso	l'intesa	the understanding
pretendere	preteso	la pretesa	the pretext, pretension
chiudere	chiuso	la chiusa	the lock
"	"	la chiusura	the closure
difendere	difeso	la difesa	the defense
offendere	offeso	l'offesa	the offense
discendere	disceso	la discesa	the descent
prendere	preso	la presa	the hold, grasp

Italian Infinitive	Italian Past Participle	Italian Noun	English Noun
imprendere	impreso	l'impresa	the undertaking
riprendere	ripreso	la ripresa	the renewal, taking up again
sorprendere	sorpreso	la sorpresa	the surprise
rendere	reso	la resa	the rendering
arrendere	arreso	l'arresa	the surrender
rispondere	risposto	la risposta	the response, reply
spendere	speso	la spesa	the expense
vedere	visto, veduto	la vista, veduta	the view
provvedere	provvisto	la provvista	the provision

A Mixed Bag of Parallel Endings

We have seen English nouns ending in -sion, -ence, -ure and the like. Usually there are corresponding Italian nouns ending in **-sione, -enza,** or **-ura,** etc., as in these examples:

Italian Infinitive	Italian Past Participle	Italian Noun	English Noun
confondere	confuso	la confusione	the confusion
dipendere	dipeso	la dipendenza	the dependence
chiudere	chiuso	la chiusura	the closure
"	"	la chiusa	the lock

You will note that the infinitives are from our **-dere** and **-ndere**) groups. Translating backward from English to Italian is generally reliable. That is, if the English noun with such an ending exists, there is usually a corresponding Italian noun. Going the other way, from Italian to English, there are several exceptions: The ending is on the Italian word but never made it to English, e.g.:

uccidere   ucciso   l'uccisione   the homicide

It is probably best for the Educated Guesser not to presume on such connections, but to check them out in the dictionary whenever in doubt.

Conspicuous by their absence thus far are verbs ending in **-gere** and **-ggere,** for instance, **dipingere** - to depict, paint and **friggere** - to fry. That's because different patterns are to be found among them than with the ones we have just been looking at. First, try the quiz coming up on the **-dere** verbs; then we will go on to the others.

Recapitulation

The next quiz will present a list of infinitives that have for the most part <u>not</u> appeared as examples thus far. For each you will be asked to supply the Italian past participle and the Italian and English nouns. If you do not know the meaning of the infinitive, look it up before going any further.

Here is a good way to attack the problem:

1. List the Italian past participle, from which <u>virtually all</u> the nouns will be derived. (Remember the Past Participle Triumphant!)

2. Ask yourself if there is a similar-sounding English noun ending in <u>-sion</u>, <u>-ence</u>, <u>-ure</u>, etc. If so, there is probably an Italian noun ending in **-sione**, **-enza**, **-ura**, etc. Plug in the nouns.

3. If there is no such English equivalent, try the feminization of the past participle, e.g.:

difendere   difeso   la difesa   the defense

4. Your intuition or prior learning may suggest an answer different from those just suggested; if so, follow your intuition.

Quiz on Second-Conjugation Verbs and Their Nouns

Italian Infinitive	Italian Past Participle	Italian Noun	English Noun
accadere			
cadere			
chiudere			
comprendere			
concedere			
concludere			
credere			
deludere			
diffondere			
evadere			
nascondere			
perdere			
persuadere			
provvedere			
richiedere			
rispondere			
sedere			
sorridere			
sospendere			
succedere			

Answers to Quiz on Second-Conjugation Nouns and Their Verbs

Italian Infinitive	Italian Past Participle	Italian Noun	English Noun
accadere	accaduto	l'accaduto	the happening
cadere	caduto	la caduta	the fall
chiudere	chiuso	la chiusa	the lock
		la chiusura	the closure
comprendere	compreso	la comprensione	the comprehension
concedere	concesso	la concessione	the concession
concludere	concluso	la conclusione	the conclusion
credere	creduto	la credenza	the credence, belief
deludere	deluso	la delusione	the disappointment (delusion a UC)
diffondere	diffuso	la diffusione	the diffusion
evadere	evaso	l'evasione	the evasion
nascondere	nascosto	il nascondiglio	the hiding place
perdere	perduto (perso)	la perdita	the loss
persuadere	persuaso	la persuasione	the persuasion
provvedere	provvisto	la provvista	the provision(s)
richiedere	richiesto	la richiesta	the request
rispondere	risposto	la risposta	the response, reply
sedere	seduto	la seduta	the seating, session
sorridere	sorriso	il sorriso	the smile
sospendere	sospeso	la sospensione	the suspension
succedere	successo	il successo	the success
		la successione	the succession

How did you do on the quiz? You should have gotten most of them right, but we threw you a few curves, too, to show that the rules are not universal.

One of the curves is that some Italian nouns are the <u>same as</u> the past participle, not the feminization of it, e.g.:

accadere	accaduto	l'accaduto
sorridere	sorriso	il sorriso

Another is that sometimes a weird ending gets tacked on for no particular reason that we can see, e.g.:

nascondere   nascosto   il nascondiglio   the hiding place

If you got around 70 to 80% right on the ones you had never seen before, obviously the rules are working well for you.

ALL OTHER ITALIAN NOUNS RELATED TO VERBS

The patterns we have just seen are also found among all other second- and third-conjugation verbs, which include the second-conjugation verbs ending in **-gere** and **-ggere**, for instance, **dipingere, friggere**. What is going to make things more difficult for the Educated Guesser is that exceptions to the patterns and rules crop up more frequently, and so the patterns lose some of their predictive value (predictive in the sense that if you know the infinitive, you can make an Educated Guess about the noun).

Nevertheless, the patterns are consistent enough that you can frequently see an Italian noun for the first time and, if you can see its resemblance to a verb, make an Educated Guess as to the meaning of the noun.

Parallel Endings

The rule that retains the greatest predictive value is that of parallel endings between English and Italian nouns. Here again is a list of the most common parallel endings, with examples for each:

Endings in -zione and -tion

Italian Infinitive	Italian Past Participle	Italian Noun	English Noun
affliggere	afflitto	l'afflizione	the affliction
eleggere	eletto	l'elezione	the election
costringere	costretto	la costrizione	the constriction
prediligere	prediletto	la predilezione	the predilection

Endings in -sione and -sion

| immergere | immerso | l'immersione | the immersion |
| sommergere | sommerso | la sommersione | the submersion |

Endings in -ezza and enza with -ness and -ence

esigere	esatto	l'esattezza	the exactness
"	"	l'esazione	the exaction (tax)
indulgere	indulto	l'indulgenza	the indulgence
apparire	apparso	l'apparenza	the appearance
preferire	preferito	la preferenza	the preference

Other Patterns

The Past Participle Triumphant. Even where there aren't any parallel endings between English and Italian, the rule of the Past Participle Triumphant is valid 90% of the time, as you will see in the examples below.

The Feminine Nearly Triumphant. This rule becomes less predictive now, because of two somewhat more frequent exceptions:

1. The past participle unchanged (stays masculine), e.g.:

piangere	pianto	il pianto	the weeping
ungere	unto	l'unto	the grease
crocifiggere	crocifisso	il crocifisso	the crucifix
prefiggere	prefisso	il prefisso	the prefix

2. The addition of **-imento** (masculine) to the stem, e.g.:

sentire	sentito	il sentimento	the sentiment
risorgere	risorto	il risorgimento	the resurgence
sconvolgere	sconvolto	lo sconvolgimento	the upset, defeat

Still, for miscellaneous other nouns, the feminine form remains the rule, as in these examples:

fingere	finto	la finta	the feint
spingere	spinto	la spinta	the push, shove
cingere	cinto	la cintura	the belt, girdle
tingere	tinto	la tinta	the tint, dye, ink
crescere	cresciuto	la crescita	the growth
uscire	uscito	l'uscita	the exit
morire	morto	la morte	the death
offrire	offerto	l'offerta	the offering
dormire	dormito	la dormita	the sleep
partire	partito	la partenza	the departure

PREPARATION FOR A FINAL QUIZ FOR THIS CHAPTER

Soon you will find a list of Italian infinitives of all three conjugations, many of them not seen previously in this chapter. Look up the meanings for any you don't recognize. Here are the tactics we suggest (a condensation of advice given before the quizzes earlier in this chapter).

First-Conjugation Verbs

For first-conjugation verbs, try:

1. Is there an English noun that has one of the usual "parallel endings"? If so, plug it in, e.g.:

spiegare   spiegato   la spiegazione   the explanation

2. If there is no such parallel ending, is the verb an intransitive verb of motion? If so, use the feminization of the past participle, e.g.:

entrare   entrato   l'entrata   the entrance

3. If it is not an intransitive verb of motion (and most of them are not), make the noun the same as the first-person singular of the verb, e.g.:

toccare   toccato   il tocco   the touch

Second-Conjugation Verbs

Verbs Ending in "-dere" and "-ndere." Does the infinitive end in **-dere** or **-ndere**? If it does, stay here; if it does not, go to "Remaining Second- and Third-Conjugation Verbs."

1. Is there an English noun that has one of the usual "parallel endings"? If so, using the Past Participle Triumphant as the stem, tack on the ending.

confondere   confuso   la confusione   the confusion

2. If there is no such parallel ending, convert the past participle into a feminine noun, e.g.:

difendere   difeso   la difesa   the defense

3. If your answer doesn't look right to you, it may be one of the miscellaneous exceptions. Put an "X" by it to show that you were suspicious.

Remaining Second- and Third-Conjugation Verbs

This is where exceptions get more numerous, once you have performed the "parallel endings" test, hence a slight change in strategy is called for.

1. Perform the "parallel endings" test. Is there an English noun that qualifies? If so, use its Italian counterpart.

indulgere	indulto	l'indulgenza	the indulgence
sommergere	sommerso	la sommersione	the submersion
impedire	impedito	l'impedimento	the impediment

2. Does some small voice tell you to make an Educated Guess that doesn't follow the most common patterns? Do you vaguely recall an **-enza**, an **-ura**, or an **-imento** that might be added on? Should the past participle stay as a masculine? If so, take that step, as shown just below; otherwise, the best odds are to go to Step 3.

partire	partito	la partenza	the departure
cingere	cinto	la cintura	the belt, girdle
risorgere	risorto	il risorgimento	the resurgence
piangere	pianto	il pianto	the weeping

3. Make the Past Participle Triumphant into a feminine noun, e.g.:

fingere	finto	la finta	the feint
spingere	spinto	la spinta	the push, shove
uscire	uscito	l'uscita	the exit
scoprire	scoperto	la scoperta	the discovery

FINAL QUIZ ON NOUNS RELATED TO VERBS

Italian Infinitive	Italian Past Participle	Italian Noun	English Noun
abbracciare	_____	_____	_____
aprire	_____	_____	_____
benedire	_____	_____	_____
bere	_____	_____	_____
comprimere	_____	_____	_____
controllare	_____	_____	_____
crescere	_____	_____	_____
decidere	_____	_____	_____
discutere	_____	_____	_____
fuggire	_____	_____	_____
girare	_____	_____	_____
imprimere	_____	_____	_____
infliggere	_____	_____	_____
notare	_____	_____	_____
occorrere	_____	_____	_____
occupare	_____	_____	_____
opporre	_____	_____	_____
praticare	_____	_____	_____
prefiggere	_____	_____	_____
procedere	_____	_____	_____
proporre	_____	_____	_____
reagire	_____	_____	_____

Italian Infinitive	Italian Past Participle	Italian Noun	English Noun
ricevere	_____	_____	_____
ridurre	_____	_____	_____
ripetere	_____	_____	_____
ritenere	_____	_____	_____
riuscire	_____	_____	_____
rompere	_____	_____	_____
salire	_____	_____	_____
scambiare	_____	_____	_____
scegliere	_____	_____	_____
scoprire	_____	_____	_____
scrivere	_____	_____	_____
servire	_____	_____	_____
spingere	_____	_____	_____
spremere	_____	_____	_____
stringere	_____	_____	_____
tagliare	_____	_____	_____
tingere	_____	_____	_____
venire	_____	_____	_____
vestire	_____	_____	_____
visitare	_____	_____	_____
volare	_____	_____	_____

Answers to Final Quiz on Nouns Related to Verbs

Italian Infinitive	Italian Past Participle	Italian Noun	English Noun
abbracciare	abbracciato	l'abbraccio	the embrace
aprire	aperto	l'apertura	the aperture, opening
benedire	benedetto	la benedizione	the benediction
bere	bevuto	la bevuta, bibita, bevanda	the beverage, drink
comprimere	compresso	la compressa	the compress, tablet
		la compressione	the compression
controllare	controllato	il controllo	the inspection
crescere	cresciuto	la crescita	the growth
decidere	deciso	la decisione	the decision
discutere	discusso	la discussione	the discussion
fuggire	fuggito	la fuga	the flight, fugue
girare	girato	il giro	the turn
imprimere	impresso	l'impressione	the impression
infliggere	inflitto	l'inflizione	the infliction
notare	notato	la nota	the note
		la notazione	the notation
occorrere	occorso	l'occorrenza	the need (occurrence a UC)
occupare	occupato	l'occupazione	the occupation
opporre	opposto	l'opposizione	the opposition
praticare	praticato	la pratica	the practice
prefiggere	prefisso	il prefisso	the prefix
procedere	processo	il processo	the judicial process
		il procedimento	the proceedings, development
		la procedura	the procedure
proporre	proposto	la proposta	the proposal
reagire	reagito	la reazione	the reaction
ricevere	ricevuto	la ricevuta	the receipt
		il ricevimento	the receiving
ridurre	ridotto	la riduzione	the reduction
ripetere	ripetuto	la ripetizione	the repetition

Italian Infinitive	Italian Past Participle	Italian Noun	English Noun
ritenere	ritenuto	la ritenuta	the belief
riuscire	riuscito	la riuscita	the success
rompere	rotto	la rottura	the rupture, break
salire	salito	la salita	the ascent, climb
scambiare	scambiato	lo scambio	the exchange
scegliere	scelto	la scelta	the choice
scoprire	scoperto	la scoperta	the discovery
scrivere	scritto	la scrittura	the writings, scripture
servire	servito	il servizio	the service
spingere	spinto	la spinta	the push, shove
spremere	spremuto	la spremuta	the squeezings (e.g., fresh juice)
stringere	stretto	la stretta	the grasp, hold
		lo stretto	the strait (geog.)
tagliare	tagliato	il taglio	the cutting
tingere	tinto	la tinta	the tint, dye, ink
venire	venuto	la venuta	the coming
vestire	vestito	il vestito	the suit, dress
visitare	visitato	la visita	the visit
volare	volato	il volo	the flight

A Final Comment

How well did you do? The answer is not to be calculated in percentages, but rather in answer to the question, "How many nouns that I had never seen before did I get right, or nearly right, because of Educated Guessing learned from this chapter?" Remember, too, of the ones you didn't get right, if you were close, the noun will be easier to recognize, remember, and reproduce the next time you need it.

TWELVE.

EFFEMINATE GREEK MASCULINES AND OTHER HELLENIC HARASSMENTS

A number of words of Greek origin are present in both English and Italian. Many of the Italian ones end in -a, e.g. **il duca -** the duke, in the singular, even though they are masculine.

English words of Greek origin that end in –sis, e.g. crisis, end with **-si** in Italian and are feminine, e.g. la **crisi**.

Academic and medical callings deriving from the Greek, while usually preserving the same root, often have quite different endings in Italian and English, e.g. **scienziato -** scientist.

This is primarily a reference chapter. Browse through it to be sure you are familiar with the rules and patterns involved and with the kinds of people and things listed. There will not be a quiz at the end of this chapter, but when you are later unsure about something covered here, come back and look it up.

EFFEMINATE MASCULINES AND UNVARYING FEMININES

Effeminate Masculines

As mentioned, there are a number of words of masculine gender that in the singular end in the usually feminine -a. In fact, many end in **-ma** or **-ta**. In the plural they nearly always end in the expected **-i**. Some of the more common of these hermaphrodites are listed below.

One thing to note is that for those nouns referring to people, e.g. **il comunista** (<u>the communist</u>) rather than things, e.g. **il clima** (<u>the climate</u>), endings for women are regular, as this example shows:

	Singular	Plural
<u>Masculine</u>	il comunista	i comunisti
<u>Feminine</u>	la comunista	le comuniste

In the list to follow, to make it simpler, only masculine forms will be given for persons (artists, communists, hermits, etc.); if you want to refer to female artists, communists, hermits, etc., use the forms shown immediately above.

Singular	Plural	Meaning
l'artista	gli artisti	the artist(s)
il cinema	i cinema*	the movie theatre(s)
il clima	i climi	the climate(s)
il collega	i colleghi	the colleague(s)
il comunista	i comunisti	the communist(s)
il dramma	i drammi	the drama(s)
il duca	i duchi	the duke(s)
l'eremita	gli eremiti	the hermit(s)
il fascista	i fascisti	the fascist(s)
il masochista	i masochisti	the masochist(s)
il monarca	i monarchi	the monarch(s)
il panorama	i panorami	the panorama(s)
il pianeta	i pianeti	the planets
il poema	i poemi	the poem(s)
il poeta	i poeti	the poet(s)
il problema	i problemi	the problem(s)
il razzista	i razzisti	the racist(s)
il sistema	i sistemi	the system(s)
il socialista	i socialisti	the socialist(s)
lo strattagemma	gli strattagemmi	the stratagem(s)
il tema	i temi	the theme(s)
il teorema	i teoremi	the theorem(s)

---

* This is one of very few of these words that does not change its ending in the plural.

Unvarying Feminines

Those words of Greek origin that end in -sis in English, e.g. analysis, synthesis, etc., are feminine in Italian and end in -si in both singular and plural, e.g. l'analisi - le analisi; la sintesi - le sintesi.

In the list below, in the column "Article," the first form given is singular, the second plural. In the column "Noun," the form shown is both singular and plural.

Article		Noun	Meaning
l'	le	analisi	the analysis(es)
l'	le	antitesi	the antithesis(es)
la	le	crisi	the crisis(es)
l'	le	ipotesi	the hypothesis(es)
la	le	paralisi	the paralysis(es)
la	le	parentesi	the parenthesis(es)
la	le	sintesi	the synthesis(es)
la	le	tesi	the thesis(es)

PROFESSIONS, PROFESSORS, AND PRACTITIONERS

The names of most academic and medical specialties and practitioners come from Greek roots, and there are many Faithful Cognates between Italian and English. Because there are enough, however, that vary between the two languages, it is wise to list them here. If you need a professor or a doctor, here is how to ask for one.

Academia

Discipline	Practitioner	Discipline	Practitioner
anthropology	anthropologist	l'antropologia	l'antropologo
architecture	architect	l'architettura	l'architetto
biology	biologist	la biologia	il biologo
chemistry	chemist	la chimica	il chimico
classics	classicist	i classici	il classicista
economics	economist	le scienze economiche	l'economista
engineering	engineer	l'ingegneria	l'ingegnere
geology	geologist	la geologia	il geologo
history	historian	la storia	lo storico
linguistics	linguist	la linguistica	il linguista

mathematics	mathematician	la matematica	il matematico
music	musician	la musica	il musicista *
philosophy	philosopher	la filosofia	il filosofo
psychology	psychologist	la psicologia	lo psicologo **
physics	physicist	la fisica	il fisico
science	scientist	la scienza	lo scienziato
sociology	sociologist	la sociologia	il sociologo
statistics	statistician	la scienza della statistica	l'esperto di statistica

Medicine

Similar inconsistences abound when naming medical specialties and practitioners. Here is how to ask for the doctor (**medico**) in Italian; for the article, for a male use **il,** for a female, use **la.**

Discipline	Practitioner	Discipline	Practitioner
anesthesiology	anesthesiologist	l'anestesia	l'anestesista
cardiology	cardiologist	la cardiologia	il cardiologo
dentistry	dentist	l'odontoiatria	il dentista
dermatology	dermatologist	la dermatologia	il dermatologo
gynecology	gynecologist	la ginecologia	il ginecologo
neurology	neurologist	la neurologia	il neurologo
obstetrics	obstetrician	l'ostetricia	l'ostetrico
orthopedics	orthopedist, orthopod	la ortopedia	l'ortopedico
pediatrics	pediatrician	la pediatria	il pediatra
psychiatry	psychiatrist	la psichiatria	lo psichiatra **
surgery	surgeon	la chirurgia	il chirurgo
urology	urologist	l'urologia	l'urologo

---

* <u>Not</u> **il musico** or **i musici,** despite the well-known group performing classical music.

** Note that words beginning **ps-** are treated as if they begin with **s-impura,** i.e. when masculine, the definite article is **lo** in the singular and **gli** in the plural.

THIRTEEN.

THE IMPERATIVE: A COMMAND PERFORMANCE

THE GIVING OF ORDERS

The imperative mode of address -- l'imperativo -- consists of giving orders. The may be given politely or sharply, but they are orders nevertheless. The word "imperative" comes from the same root as "imperial," "imperious," and "emporer." Giving orders is clearly the order of the day.

There are <u>positive</u> and <u>negative</u> imperatives. We mention this distinction now because there are slight differences in the rules by that they are formed in Italian. A positive imperative instructs someone to do something: "Go to the store!" A negative imperative forbids: "Don't step in the puddle!"

In English

In English, in the singular, the only imperative is in the second person: "Go to the store!," "Do your homework!," "Tell me what happened!" Usually the subject pronoun "You" is understood, though it is sometimes used for emphasis: "<u>You</u> go to the store!," "<u>You</u> do your homework!," etc. If a "Please" is attached, the peremptory tone is softened: "Please go to the store!"

In the first-person plural, the sentence usually starts with "Let's": "Let's go to the beach," "Let's play some frisbee," etc. In the second-person plural, where two or more people are being addressed, it is formed as in the second person singular: "You (all) go to the store!," "You (all) do your homework!," etc.

There is no first-person singular imperative. If you are mentally giving yourself an order, "Go to bed, idiot, because you have to get up early in the morning!," you are treating the order-receiving part of yourself as a second-person singular.

In English, there aren't any third-person imperatives, singular or plural.

In Italian

In Italian there are all the forms there are in English, and there are the third-person singular and plural forms, too. They are used exactly as when one uses the **tu** and **Lei** forms in the indicative: One uses the second-person forms with people with whom one is familiar and would use **tu** or **voi**, and one uses the third-person forms where a certain amount of formality is called for and where one would use **Lei** or **Loro**.

FORMING THE POSITIVE IMPERATIVE

Inspect Table 13.1, in which the indicative and the imperative for each of the three conjugations, each with a sample regular and irregular verb, is given.

The first thing to note is that there is no first-person singular imperative, as we mentioned above.

The second thing to note is that there are minor changes of vowels (minor, perhaps, but they have to be learned, nevertheless) between the indicative endings and those of the imperative, in several of the forms.

The third thing to note is that the first- and second-persons plural do not change between the two modes: Indicative and imperative are the same.

The fourth thing to note, for the irregular verbs, is this important rule:

> The irregularity in the first-person singular in the indicative is mirrored in the third persons, singular and plural, in the imperative. *

---

* The imperative is largely derived from its Latin origins in the subjunctive. When we get to the subjunctive, you will notice many forms similar to those you see here.

TABLE 13.1: THE INDICATIVE AND THE IMPERATIVE

FIRST CONJUGATION

A Regular Verb: Parlare

Indicative	Imperative
parlo	---
parli	parla
parla	parli
parliamo	parliamo
parlate	parlate
parlano	parlino

An Irregular Verb: Andare

Indicative	Imperative
vado	---
vai	va' (vai)
va	vada
andiamo	andiamo
andate	andate
vanno	vadano

SECOND CONJUGATION

A Regular Verb: Credere

Indicative	Imperative
credo	---
credi	credi
crede	creda
crediamo	crediamo
credete	credete
credono	credano

An Irregular Verb: Tenere

Indicative	Imperative
tengo	---
tieni	tieni
tiene	tenga
teniamo	teniamo
tenete	tenete
tengono	tengano

THIRD CONJUGATION

A Regular Verb: Dormire

Indicative	Imperative
dormo	---
dormi	dormi
dorme	dorma
dormiamo	dormiamo
dormite	dormite
dormono	dormano

An Irregular Verb: Capire

Indicative	Imperative
capisco	---
capisci	capisci
capisce	capisca
capiamo	capiamo
capite	capite
capiscono	capiscano

Let's take a moment to ponder this fourth thing further, because if you understand it you will save yourself a lot of grief in forming imperatives for irregular verbs.

Let's take a look at **andare**. The first-person singular in the indicative is **vado**. The third-persons, singular and plural, in the imperative are **vada** and **vadano**, respectively. Thus the root, **vad-**, is preserved in both those imperative forms.

Now look at **tenere**. There is an intrusive "g" in the first-person singular indicative, namely **tengo**. That same intrusive "g" shows up in the third persons in the imperative, namely, **tenga** and **tengano**.

Finally to **capire**, an **-isco** verb, as shown in the first-person singular indicative, **capisco**. Again, see the **-isc-** stem preserved in the third persons imperative, namely, **capisca** and **capiscano**.

Do you have this <u>fourth</u> thing down cold? If not, go back over the material until you are sure you understand it! It is <u>very</u> useful!

A <u>fifth</u> thing to note is that the second-person singular imperative for **andare** is spelt **va'**, but is pronounced **vai**, just as is the indicative. So if you want to tell a friend or a dog to "Go away!," you speak the words, **"Vai via!"** This will also turn out to be true for **fare** and **dare**: The words are spelt **fa'** and **da'**, but pronounced **fai** and **dai**, respectively.

Using the Imperative: 1. For Regular Verbs

Once you have mastered the new sets of verb endings for the imperative, you can start giving orders. Three regular verbs frequently used in the imperative are: **guardare** (to look at), **attendere** (to wait), and **sentire** (to listen to). Following are some examples.

In English, when we want to call attention to something, we will often say, "Look!" or "Look at that!," indicating where the respondent should look. In Italian, to a friend, one usually says, **"Guarda!"**; to a stranger, one says, **"Guardi!"** If an interesting program is on television and I want my friend to look at it, I'll say to him, **"Guarda la televisione!"**

When you want someone to wait, use either **aspettare** or **attendere.** Years ago, when I worked in Genova, if I wanted to telephone out of the clinic, I would dial the **portiere,** who presided over the outgoing phone lines, and ask for "**una linea, per favore.**" If the well-spoken Domenico were on duty, he would say, "**Attenda** un attimo, professore, per favore." ("Wait a moment, please, professor.") One of his colleagues would say, "**Aspetti** un attimo, professore," but **attenda** was clearly Domenico's favorite.

In English, if we want to catch someone's attention, we will often say, "Listen!," or "Listen to this!" or, less elegantly, "Hey!" The Italians use the verb **sentire** for this purpose (and it has many other uses, too). If you have an important bit of gossip for your friend, you say, "**Senti,** Giovanni." ("Listen, Giovanni."). If you want to get the attention of the lady sitting next to you on the bus, perhaps to tell her that a black widow spider is crawling up her leg, you would say, "**Senta,** signora, per favore." ("Listen, ma'am, please.").

Using the Imperative: 2. For Irregular Verbs

Two incidents have always made the polite form of the imperative of two important irregular verbs, **andare** and **venire,** easy for me to remember.

One cold, autumn evening I was taking the bus from Genova to Nervi. Standing at the rear of the bus, near the ticket taker, was a young couple, holding hands and smooching. The ticket taker was most disapproving and asked the boy several times to stop. The couple ignored him. When the bus stopped at the piazza in Nervi, the doors opened and the couple started to step out. The ticket taker said to the boy, in a barely controlled rage, "Vada via! Vada, **vada,** VADA!!!" The ticket taker learned that it is hard to interfere with young love, and I learned that the third-person singular imperative of **andare** is **vada.**

On another occasion, we had entered a restaurant, and the maitre d' had indicated we should wait for a few minutes for a table to clear. When he turned to us a little while later, he was about ten feet away and made a gesture similar to that which Americans use to mean "Stay put!" when playing capture-the-flag or soldiers. At the same time, he kept saying, "**Venga, venga.**" We didn't know that the gesture to an Italian means, "Come along; follow me," nor did I know with my primitive Italian at the time that **venga** is the polite imperative of **venire.** He soon realized that we did not comprehend his message, came up to us and explained that our table was ready. And I soon realized that the polite imperative of **venire** is **venga.**

Both of these incidents demonstrate the rule that the first-person singular in the indicative is the stem of the third-person singular in the imperative:

vado - **vad**a!   I <u>go.</u> - You (polite) <u>go!</u>
vengo - **veng**a!   I <u>come.</u> - You (polite) <u>come!</u>

Using the Imperative: 3. Where Pronouns Go

Imperatives are often used with a pronoun, e.g. "Tell <u>me</u>," "Excuse <u>me</u>," "Please, make <u>yourself</u> comfortable," etc.

In English, the pronoun always follows the verb, as in the examples just shown. In Italian, it follows the verb if you are using the second person, **tu** or **voi**, but it precedes the verb if you are using the third person, **Lei** or **Loro**. Here are some examples of imperative cast in the second person and then in the third:

1. **Scusami**, Paolo. <u>Excuse me</u>, Paolo.
   Mi scusi, signore, per favore. Please <u>excuse me</u>, sir.

2. **Dimmi**, Giovanna. <u>Tell me</u>, Giovanna.
   Mi dica, signora, la prego. <u>Tell me</u>, ma'am, please.

3. **Accomodati**, Giuseppe. <u>Seat yourself</u> (<u>make yourself</u> <u>comfortable</u>), Giuseppe.

   Prego, professore, **si accomodi**. Please, professor, <u>seat</u> <u>yourself</u> (<u>make yourself comfortable</u>).

We have chosen these three verbs -- **scusare, dire, accomodarsi** -- because they are very frequently heard. The Italians are very polite, and if there is a chance that someone has given offense -- perhaps brushed against you too hard in a crowded bus -- the phrase **"Mi scusi"** is almost inevitable.

The second example, **dimmi**, involves a construction called "geminization," the doubling up of ("making twins out of") a consonant, which sometimes happens in Italian when two words are being combined. This use of geminization in the imperative occurs when you are using the **tu** form of the verbs **andare, dare, fare,** or **dire,** and a pronoun is involved. The full conjugation of these latter three verbs and three other irregular verbs, **avere, essere,** and **volere,** in both indicative and imperative is found in Table 13.2; that for **andare** is in Table 13.1.

TABLE 13.2: THE INDICATIVE AND IMPERATIVE OF AVERE, ESSERE, DARE, DIRE, FARE, AND VOLERE

Indicative	Imperative	Indicative	Imperative
avere		**essere**	
ho	---	sono	---
hai	abbi	sei	sii
ha	abbia	è	sia
abbiamo	abbiamo	siamo	siamo
avete	abbiate	siete	siate
hanno	abbiano	sono	siano
dare		**dire**	
do	---	dico	---
dai	da' (dai)	dici	di'
dà	dia	dice	dica
diamo	diamo	diciamo	diciamo
date	date	dite	dite
danno	diano	dicono	dicano
fare		**volere**	
faccio	---	voglio	---
fai	fa' (fai)	vuoi	vogli
fa	faccia	vuole	voglia
facciamo	facciamo	vogliamo	vogliamo
fate	fate	volete	vogliate
fanno	facciano	vogliono	vogliano

Some Other Common Usages

"Get to the Point; Give!"   When someone is slow in getting to the point, the impatient listener will often say, **"Da', da'"** (pronounced "Dai, dai"), meaning "Give, give."

"Stop it!" When an Italian mother is exasperated by the behavior of a mischievous child, she will say, "**Smettila!**," from the verb **smettere**, to stop doing something, to cease. In case that doesn't work, she will say, "**Piantala!**," literally, "Plant it!," but meaning "Stop it!." (The reason the pronoun "it" is **la** rather than the more common **lo** is because it refers to "the action," the feminine **l'azione**.)

Women receiving unwanted attentions from men should use the polite, third-person form -- "**La smetta!**" -- to repel impolite behavior. If they use the familiar, second-person construction, they may encourage even greater familiarities.

"Let's go!" "**Andiamo!**" is a well-known Italian imperative. "Let's go to the beach!" "**Andiamo alla spiaggia!**"

The General Imperative

All the imperatives we have shown thus far have been directed to specific people. Often notices to the general public, where the object of the imperative is indefinite, use the infinitive as an imperative. Above a tricky flight of stairs you may see a sign saying: **Fare Attenzione**.

FORMING THE NEGATIVE IMPERATIVE

The General Imperative

In notices to the public, usually the simple addition of **non** to the infinitive does the trick, and you have a negative general imperative.

Over the doors of every bus in Italy there is this sign:

Non Ingombrare L'Uscita
Don't Block (Encumber) the Exit

Immediately under the sign are usually several Italians, blocking the exit. So much for respect for governmental edict. (Note also that **ingombrare** and encumber are QC's.)

The Particular Imperative

For negative commands given to specific people, add **non** to the positive imperative in all cases but the second-person singular, where you use the infinitive. Here is the negative imperative for **parlare**:

---	non parliamo
non parlare	non parlate
non parli	non parlino

QUIZ ON IMPERATIVES

In the sentences below, the familiar form of address will be shown by the use of first names, e.g. Elena, Carlo, etc. The polite form will be shown by use of titles, e.g. signora, professore, etc. Translate the sentences, then check against the answers that follow on page 132.

1. Carlo, please look for the book.

   _____

2. Please be seated, signora.

   _____

3. Elena and Carlo, please go to the store.

   _____

4. Come with me, please, professor.

   _____

5. Gianni, don't look at television now.

   _____

6. Sir, please wait a moment.

   _____

7. Paolo and Maria, please finish your homework.

   _____

8. Let's go to the theatre.

   _____

9. Gianni, tell me what you think.

   _____

10. Carlo, listen.

    _____

11. Non ingombrare l'uscita.

_____

12. Ragazzo, vai via.

_____

13. Elena, fammelo vedere.

_____

14. Marcello, smettila.

_____

15. Carlo, non parlare di queste cose.

_____

16. Mi scusi, per favore, signora.

_____

17. Dimmi, Gianni.

_____

18. Mi dica, dottore.

_____

19. Vieni qua, Carlo.

_____

20. Maria, non entrare.

_____

Answers to Quiz on Imperatives

1. Carlo, please look for the book.
   Carlo, per favore, **cerca** il libro.

2. Please, ma'am, be seated.
   Prego, signora, **si accomodi**.

3. Elena and Carlo, please go to the store.
   Elena e Carlo, **andate** al negozio, per favore.

4. Come with me, please, professor.
   Venga con me, per favore, professore.

5. Gianni, don't look at television now.
   Gianni, **non guardare** la televisione adesso.

6. Sir, please wait a moment.
   Signore, per favore, **attenda (aspetti)** un attimo.

7. Paolo and Maria, please finish your homework.
   Paolo e Maria, per piacere, **finite** il vostro compito.

8. Let's go to the theatre.
   Andiamo al teatro.

9. Gianni, tell me what you think.
   Gianni, **dimmi** che cosa pensi.

10. Carlo, listen.
    Carlo, **senti**.

11. Non ingombrare l'uscita.
    Don't block (encumber) the exit.

12. Ragazzo, vai via.
    Young man, go away.

13. Elena, fammelo vedere.
    Elena, let me see it.

14. Marcello, smettila.
    Marcello, stop it.

15. Carlo, non parlare di queste cose.
    Carlo, don't talk about these things.

16. Mi scusi, per favore, signora.
    Excuse me, please, ma'am.

17. Dimmi, Gianni.
    Tell me, Gianni.

18. Mi dica, dottore.
    Tell me, doctor.

19. Vieni qua, Carlo.
    Come here, Carlo.

20. Maria, non entrare.
    Maria, don't come in.

THE CONDITIONAL AS A POLITE IMPERATIVE

The Conditional Mood

The conditional mood is one where an element of doubt enters, in contrast to the affirmative tone of the <u>indicative</u>, as shown in these examples:

<u>Indicative</u>

It <u>will</u> rain today.

I <u>will go</u> to the store today.

I <u>want</u> a glass of water.

He <u>can</u> read the book.

<u>Conditional</u>

It <u>might</u> rain today.

I <u>would go</u> to the store today (if you would go with me).

I <u>would like</u> a glass of water (if you would get it).

He <u>could read</u> the book (if he could stay awake).

In these examples, the <u>conditional verb</u> (might, would, could) is dependent on an implied or explicit condition, e.g. "if you would go with me," "if you would get it," "if he could stay awake."

Polite Imperatives

In both English and Italian, putting the auxiliary verbs <u>to be able to</u>, <u>can</u> (**potere**) and <u>to want</u>, <u>will</u> (**volere**) in the conditional softens their imperious tone when they are used as an apparent request but are really polite imperatives. In the following examples the sentence will first be given in the indicative, then in the conditional as a polite imperative:

1. <u>Can</u> I have a glass of water?
   Posso avere un bicchiere d'acqua?

   <u>Could</u> (<u>May</u>) I have a glass of water?
   Potrei avere un bicchiere d'acqua?

2. I <u>want</u> to order.
   Voglio ordinare.

   I <u>would like</u> to order.
   Vorrei ordinare.

3. Sir, <u>can</u> you tell me what time it is?
   Signore, **può** dirmi l'ora?

   Sir, <u>could</u> you tell me what time it is?
   Signore, **potrebbe** dirmi che ore sono?

The Indicative and Conditional for **Potere** and **Volere**

Indicative	Conditional	Indicative	Conditional
posso	potrei	voglio	vorrei
puoi	potresti	vuoi	vorresti
può	potrebbe	vuole	vorrebbe
possiamo	potremmo	vogliamo	vorremmo
potete	potreste	volete	vorreste
possono	potrebbero	vogliono	vorrebbero

Quiz on Conditional as Polite Imperative

Translate the following sentences, using the conditional. Check your work against the answers on page 135.

1. Waiter, could you come here, please?

_____

2. Maria and Elena, could you come to dinner tonight?

_____

3. I would like (to have) a cigarette. Sir, could you please give me a cigarette?

_____

_____

4. May (can) I speak with Luigi?

_____

5. Carlo, could you please go to the store for me?

_____

6. Elena, could you give me more wine?

_____

7. Elena, would you like more wine?

_____

8. Giacomo, could you please finish your homework?

_____

Answers to Quiz on the Conditional as Polite Imperative

1. Waiter, could you come here, please?
   Cameriere, **potrebbe venire** qua, per favore?

2. Maria and Elena, could you come to dinner tonight?
   Maria e Elena, **potreste venire** a cena con noi stasera?

3. I would like (to have) a cigarette.
   Vorrei (avere) una sigaretta.

   Sir, could you please give me a cigarette?
   Signore, **potrebbe darmi** una sigaretta?

4. May (can) I speak with Luigi?
   Potrei parlare con Luigi?

5. Carlo, could you please go to the store for me?
   Carlo, **potresti andare** per me al negozio, per favore?

6. Elena, could you give me more wine?
   Elena, **potresti darmi** ancora un po' di vino?

7. Elena, would you like more wine?
   Elena, **vorresti** un'altro po' di vino?

8. Giacomo, could you please finish your homework?
   Giacomo, **potresti finire** il compito?

FOURTEEN.

YESTERDAY, TODAY, AND TOMORROW: EXPRESSIONS OF TIME

There is a multitude of expressions involving time, e.g. "When we were very young," "Get me to the church on time," "From this moment on," etc. which tell when something happens. In Italian, as in English, many of these expressions are used idiomatically and have to be seen in the context of a sentence if one is to make proper use of them.

Later in the chapter, we will list over 40 expressions, all of them embedded in a phrase or sentence to give proper context. We have gathered them here in a single chapter so that you can use it as a reference section. Look it over now, to familiarize yourself with its contents, but please promise that you won't try to memorize anything. Wait till you are trying to express a concept involving time, then come back here to find the word or phrase that best does the job.

Before we go to the expressions themselves, you will be introduced to two new verb tenses: the <u>imperfect</u> and the <u>future</u>. You will need to know them and when to use them for the expressions of time. So there will first be a brief digression into "A Little Grammar."

A LITTLE GRAMMAR

In the chapter "Don't Get Tensed Up about Tenses," we suggested you defer until later learning such tenses as the _imperfect_ and the _future_. The day of reckoning has arrived. It is now necessary for you to learn them if you are to use expressions of time correctly.

The Imperfect — **L'Imperfetto**

<u>When the Imperfect Is Called For</u>. The imperfect tense -- l'imperfetto -- is the form of the past tense that shows the following:

1. States of being and feeling, e.g. "When I was young," "He was sad," "The war raged for years."

2. Enduring qualities, e.g. "He was a man of integrity," "Spring was always a season of hope," "The lights of Naples were beautiful."

3. Repeated actions, e.g. "He went to church every Sunday," "I used to go butterfly hunting," "She got up early every morning."

4. Continuity of action, often introduced in clauses starting with "while" or "when," e.g. "While the others were talking," "When he lived in Rome," "As they walked down the street."

These examples stand in contrast to the uses of the **passato prossimo** (recent past or present perfect) we studied earlier. In the **passato prossimo**, we described <u>completed actions</u>, things that were done once, or several times, but were over and completed. Sometimes both tenses will be used in a single sentences, as in these examples:

1. When I <u>was</u> (state of being) a youth, I <u>had</u> blond hair (enduring quality).

Quando **ero** (imperfetto) giovane, **avevo** (imperfetto) i capelli biondi.

2. I <u>kept telling</u> (repeated action) him that it <u>was</u> (state of being) a bad idea.

Gli **dicevo** (imperfetto) che **era** (imperfetto) una brutta idea.

3. He <u>was</u> (state of feeling) happy when he <u>heard</u> (completed action) the news.

Era (imperfetto) contento quando **ha sentito** (passato prossimo) le notizie.

4. While we <u>were living</u> (continuity) in Genova, we <u>met</u> (completed action) many nice people.

   Mentre **abitavamo** (imperfetto) a Genova, **abbiamo conosciuto** (passato prossimo) molta gente simpatica.

5. He <u>used to play</u> (continuing action) tennis; but then he <u>had</u> (completed action) the accident.

   Giocava (imperfetto) a tennis; ma poi **ha avuto** (passato prossimo) l'incidente.

<u>How to Form the Imperfect</u>. For the three conjugations, lop off the ending of the infinitive and add the specific endings, just as you did when learning the present tense. Note that the endings are similar for the three conjugations; only the vowel changes according to the conjugation.

For once, our often irregular -isco verbs are <u>not</u> irregular. They form the imperfect in the same way that other third conjugation verbs do. The first-person imperfect for cap**i**re is cap/**ivo**; that for dorm**i**re is dorm/**ivo**.

Essere continues to be maddeningly irregular, as usual, but for once even **avere** is regular.

Here are the imperfects for **essere**, **avere**, and for the three conjugations.

Essere	Avere	Parlare	Credere	Dormire
ero	avevo	parl/**avo**	cred/**evo**	dorm/**ivo**
eri	avevi	parl/**avi**	cred/**evi**	dorm/**ivi**
era	aveva	parl/**ava**	cred/**eva**	dorm/**iva**
eravamo	avevamo	parl/**avamo**	cred/**evamo**	dorm/**ivamo**
eravate	avevate	parl/**avate**	cred/**evate**	dorm/**ivate**
erano	avevano	parl/**avano**	cred/**evano**	dorm/**ivano**

The Future — **Il Futuro**

<u>When the Future Is Called For</u>. The future in Italian is used much as it is in English. It refers to events that definitely or very probably will take place in the future, e.g. "He will start school next week." (If the future event might well not happen, that is, if one is speculating, e.g. "He might start school next week," one uses the subjunctive in Italian. But the subjunctive is a can of worms best left unopened at this point; we will open it when we must, toward the end of the book.)

How to Form the Future. Here are **essere**, **avere**, and the three conjugations in the future. As usual the first two are irregular. The three conjugations merely have a new set of endings to tack on to the stem of the infinitive.

Essere	Avere	Parlare	Credere	Dormire
sarò	avrò	parl/**erò**	cred/**erò**	dorm/**irò**
sarai	avrai	parl/**erai**	cred/**erai**	dorm/**irai**
sarà	avrà	parl/**erà**	cred/**erà**	dorm/**irà**
saremo	avremo	parl/**eremo**	cred/**eremo**	dorm/**iremo**
sarete	avrete	parl/**erete**	cred/**erete**	dorm/**irete**
saranno	avranno	parl/**eranno**	cred/**eranno**	dorm/**iranno**

THE EXPRESSIONS OF TIME

You will probably be thinking in English when you want to use one of these expressions, e.g. "How do I say 'ever since' in Italian?" For that reason, we will list the expressions first in English, then in Italian. The key word or phrase in each expression will be stated and then an example will follow.

The lists will be presented in the following categories: past, present, future, and miscellaneous. Within each of the categories, the items will be presented in alphabetical order in English.

The Past — **Il Passato**

1. after

   dopo

   <u>After</u> the exam, I went to bed.

   Dopo l'esame, sono andato a letto.

2. ago

   fa

   I came to Italy many years <u>ago</u>.

   Sono venuto in Italia molti anni **fa**.

3. as

   da

   <u>As</u> a child, I had blond hair.

   Da piccolo, avevo i capelli biondi.

4. before

   prima (di)

   I usually get up <u>before</u> seven o'clock.

   Di solito mi alzo **prima delle** sette.

5. ever since, from

   fin da

   <u>Ever since</u> he was 20, he smoked too much.

   Fin da quando aveva 20 anni, ha fumato troppo.

6. for the past

He has been studying Italian <u>for the past</u> three weeks.

da +
(present tense)

Lui **studia** italiano **da** tre settimane.

7. from one time to the next

The team was never the same <u>from one time to the next</u>.

di volta in volta, da una volta all'altra

La squadra non era mai la stessa **di volta in volta (da una volta all'altra)**.

8. last (final)

That was the <u>last</u> year he was able to go.

ultimo

Quello è stato **l'ultimo** anno in cui è potuto andare.

9. last (most recent)

<u>Last</u> week he didn't come.

scorso, passato

La settimana **scorsa (passata)** non è venuto.

10. last (of a series)

You paid for the beer <u>last time</u>.

l'ultima volta

Hai pagato la birra **l'ultima volta**.

11. since, from the time when

<u>Since (from the time when)</u> he was six, he has been in school

da quando +
(present tense) OR

Va a scuola **da quando** aveva sei anni.

da (time) **in poi**
+ (present perfect)

Dai sei anni **in poi, è andato** a scuola.

12. then (after that)

He got up, and <u>then</u> he ate.

poi

Si è alzato e **poi** ha mangiato.

13. then (at that time)

I was 26 years old <u>then</u>.

allora

Avevo 26 anni **allora**.

14. years old (be)

I was 26 <u>years old</u> then.

avere anni

Avevo 26 anni allora.

15. yesterday

We ate at a restaurant <u>yesterday</u>.

ieri

Abbiamo mangiato al ristorante **ieri**.

The Present — **Il Presente**

16. from now on,   From now on, I will write every day.
    henceforth

    da ora in poi   Da **ora in poi**, scrivo ogni giorno.

17. hitherto, until now   Until now space travel was a dream.

    finora,   **Finora (fino ad oggi)**, il viaggio
    fino ad oggi   nella spazio era un sogno.

18. now, currently   I'm going home now.

    ora, adesso   **Ora (adesso)** vado a casa.

19. still, yet   Are you still hungry?

    ancora   Hai fame **ancora**?

29. the time is ...   What time is it? It's three o'clock.

    le ore sono ... Che **ore sono**? **Sono le tre**.

30. today   The weather is beautiful today.

    oggi   Fa bel tempo **oggi**.

The Future — **Il Futuro**

31. day after tomorrow   Franco will be here the day after tomorrow.

    dopodomani   Franco sarà qui **dopodomani**.

32. in   I will go home in five minutes.

    fra, tra   **Fra (tra)** cinque minuti vado a casa.

33. next (imminent)   I am going to Florence next week.

    prossimo   Vado a Firenze la **prossima** settimana.

34. next (in order),   He will leave the day after.
    after

    successivo, dopo   Partirà il giorno **successivo (dopo)**.

35. soon, in a little while	Franco will be here <u>soon</u>.
presto; fra poco	Franco sarà qui **presto (fra poco)**.
36. tomorrow	Franco will be here <u>tomorrow</u>.
domani	Franco sarà qui **domani**.
37. within	I have to sell the car <u>within</u> six months.
entro	Devo vendere la macchina **entro** sei mesi.

Miscellaneous — Miscellaneo

38. at (the time, hour)	<u>At</u> 10:00 a.m.
alle + (o'clock)	**Alle** dieci del mattino.
39. century	This is the twentieth <u>century</u>.
secolo	Questo è il ventesimo **secolo**.
40. day	Franco will be here within two <u>days</u>.
giorno	Franco sarà qui fra due **giorni**.

41. day by day
    (non-progressive
    sense)
	This job is to be done <u>day by day</u>.

giorno per giorno	Questo è un compito da farsi **giorno per giorno**.
42. day by day (progressive sense)	His Italian is improving <u>day by day</u>.
di giorno in giorno	Il suo Italiano migliora **di giorno in giorno**.
43. early (in general)	The train is <u>early</u>.
in anticipo	Il treno è **in anticipo**.
44. early (of a clock)	The clock is <u>fast</u> (<u>early</u>).
avanti	L'orologio è **avanti**.
45. fortnight, two weeks	Franco will be here in <u>two weeks</u>.
quindici giorni	Franco sarà qui fra **quindici giorni**.

46. from time to time	I read mystery stories <u>from time to time</u>.
ogni tanto, di tanto in tanto	Leggo i libri gialli **ogni tanto** (**di tanto in tanto**).
47. from (this hour) to (that hour)	He is in his office <u>from</u> 9:00 a.m. <u>to</u> noon.
fra - e; da - a	Lui è nel suo ufficio **fra** le nove e mezzogiorno.
	Lui è nel suo ufficio **dalle** nove **a** mezzogiorno.
48. late (general)	I'm sorry I'm <u>late</u> this morning.
in ritardo	Mi dispiace di essere **in ritardo** stamattina.
49. late (of a clock)	This clock is <u>slow</u> (<u>late</u>).
indietro	Quest'orologio è **indietro**.
50. moment	I'll be there in a <u>moment</u>.
attimo, momento	Sarò là fra un **attimo** (**momento**).
51. month	This is the <u>month</u> of July.
mese	Questo è il **mese** di Luglio.
52. on time (person)	Paul is <u>on time</u>.
puntuale	Paolo è **puntuale**.
53. on time (vehicle)	The train is <u>on time</u>.
in orario ("on schedule")	Il treno è **in orario**.
54. quarter of an hour	The train is a <u>quarter of an hour</u> late.
quarto d'ora	Il treno è in ritardo un **quarto d'ora** (ha un **quarto d'ora** di ritardo.)
55. week	Today is the first day of the <u>week</u>.
settimana	Oggi è il primo giorno della **settimana**.
56. year	We'll be in Italy for a <u>year</u>.
anno	Saremo in Italia per un **anno**.

A BUSY MONTH

In one of our classroom sessions during 1981, Prof. G. R. Orvieto of the **Università per Stranieri** (Perugia) helped clarify the use of many of these terms by a series of examples all involving "**un mese**." Virtually all the examples could of course be recast using **un giorno, dieci minuti, un anno**, etc., but we'll stick with Prof. Orvieto's presentation.

fra un mese
un mese **fa**

da un mese
è un mese **che**

in un mese
entro un mese

dopo un mese
un mese **dopo**

per un mese

un mese **prima**
prima di un mese

The first two, **fra** and **fa**, both express an exact time in the future or past, respectively. **Fra un mese** means exactly a month from now, not tomorrow or next week. **Un mese fa** means exactly a month ago, not yesterday or a week ago, e.g.:

Mio fratello arriverà **fra un mese**.
My brother will arrive <u>in (exactly) a month</u>.

Mio fratello è arrivato **un mese fa**.
My brother arrived <u>(exactly) a month ago</u>.

Da un mese and **è un mese che** both suggest something that has been going on for a month and continues to the present; the second is more forceful, e.g.:

Studio qui **da un mese**.
I study (have been studying) here <u>for a month</u>.

È un mese che ti aspetto!
<u>It is (has been) a month</u> I wait (have been waiting) for you!

In un mese refers to the entire period of a month, something that occupies a whole month, e.g.:

Ho scritto questo articolo **in un mese**.
I wrote this article <u>in a month</u>.
(This implies it took a whole month to write the article.)

Entro un mese means <u>within a month</u>, and can refer to tomorrow, next week or, at the latest, 31 days from now, e.g.:

Devo vendere la macchina **entro un mese**.
I have to sell the car <u>within a month</u>.

Thus, "Parto **fra** un mese" and "Parto **entro** un mese" mean, respectively, "I'm leaving <u>exactly</u> a month from now" and "I'm leaving <u>sometime within</u> this next month."

Dopo un mese implies something happened <u>after a month had elapsed</u>, whereas **un mese dopo** implies the month that came after something had happened, e.g.:

Dopo un mese a Roma, sono partito per Nizza.
<u>After a month</u> in Rome, I left for Nice.

Lui è arrivato **un mese dopo** la tua partenza.
He arrived <u>a month after</u> your departure.

Per un mese can refer to an undetermined month, one that has not yet been fixed, e.g.:

Andiamo in montagna **per un mese** quest'estate.
We're going to the mountains this summer <u>for a month</u>.

Un mese prima means <u>a month before</u> something happened, making it symmetrical with **un mese dopo** (<u>a month after</u>). But **prima di un mese** is used with prepositional phrases, to mean <u>before the month</u>, e.g.:

Un mese prima, Paola era molta ammalata.
<u>A month before</u>, Paola was very sick.

Prima di un mese non avrò la risposta.
I will not have the answer <u>before a month</u> from now.

One further note: Italians count today in estimates of the future. Thus **quindici giorni** (15 days) refers to the same two weeks away from now as <u>a fortnight</u> means in English. Likewise, **oggi a otto** means <u>a week from now</u> and **oggi a un mese** means <u>a month from now</u> as does **un mese oggi**.

QUIZ ON EXPRESSIONS OF TIME

Two Points of View

We said at the beginning of this chapter not to study it, but to use it instead as a reference. So don't take this quiz until you have <u>used</u> this chapter a bit, if you want to use it as a test of your knowledge.

Sometimes quizzes can serve as a spur to acquiring knowledge, and this one could serve that purpose for you. The sentences given employ many of the terms just listed. If you take the quiz and study the items you miss, you can start using many of these expressions right away.

The Quiz

Translate into the other language; expressions of time will be underlined in both the questions and the answers that follow.

1. <u>Before going</u> to class, I ought to (must) study.

   _____

2. They were happy <u>after</u> the rain had stopped.

   _____

3. <u>From time to time</u> I wake up early.

   _____

4. The game will end <u>in</u> two minutes.

   _____

5. The plane arrived fifteen minutes <u>ago</u>.

   _____

6. I <u>kept going back</u> (**tornare**) into the water because it <u>was</u> so hot.

   _____

7. He <u>used to play tennis</u>, <u>until</u> he had the accident.

   _____

8. The lesson lasts one <u>hour</u>, <u>from</u> nine <u>to</u> ten.

   _____

9. <u>Da quando è stato</u> in Italia, vuole tornare a Firenze.

_____

10. <u>Fin dall'ultima settimana</u>, ha mangiato molto.

_____

11. Guardo la televisione <u>da sei ore</u>.

_____

12. <u>Da ora in poi</u>, ti prometto di stare zitto (stay quiet).

_____

13. <u>Da piccolo, ero</u> molto grasso.

_____

14. <u>Dopo aver trovato</u> i gettoni (phone coins), ho telefonato alla mia mamma.

_____

15. "<u>Quanti anni hai?</u>" "Ne <u>ho</u> ventuno."

_____

16. "Lei non è <u>più</u> qui?" "No, Lei è partita due <u>mesi fa</u>."

_____

Answers to Quiz on Expressions of Time

1. <u>Before going</u> to class, I ought to (must) study.

   Prima di andare in classe, devo studiare.

2. They were happy <u>after</u> the rain had stopped.

   Loro erano contenti **dopo che** la pioggia era cessata.

3. <u>From time to time</u> I wake up early.

   Ogni tanto mi sveglio presto.

4. The game will end <u>in</u> two minutes.

   La partita finirà **fra (tra)** due minuti.

5. The plane arrived fifteen minutes <u>ago</u>.

   L'aeroplano è arrivato quindici minuti **fa.**

6. I <u>kept going back</u> (**tornare**) into the water because it <u>was</u> so hot.

   Tornavo nell'acqua perchè **faceva** molto caldo.

7. He <u>used to play</u> tennis, <u>until</u> he had the accident.

   Giocava a tennis, **fino a** ha avuto l'incidente.

8. The lesson lasts one <u>hour</u>, <u>from</u> nine <u>to</u> ten.

   La lezione dura **un ora, dalle** nove **alle** dieci (**fra** le nove **e** le dieci).

9. **Da quando è stato** in Italia, vuole tornare a Firenze.

   <u>Ever since he was</u> in Italy, he has wanted to go back to Florence.

10. **Fin dall'ultima settimana,** ha mangiato molto.

    <u>Ever since last week</u>, he has eaten a lot.

11. Guardo la televisione **da sei ore.**

    I've been watching the television <u>for six hours.</u>

12. **Da ora in poi,** ti prometto di stare zitto (stay quiet).

    <u>From now on,</u> I promise you I'll stay quiet.

13. **Da piccolo, ero** molto grasso.

    <u>As a child, I was</u> fat.

14. **Dopo aver trovato** i gettoni (phone coins), ho telefonato alla mia mamma.

    <u>After having found (finding)</u> the coins, I called my mother.

15. **"Quanti anni hai?"** "Ne **ho** ventuno."

    <u>"How old are you?"</u> "I <u>am</u> twenty-one." (Of them -- years -- <u>I have</u> twenty-one.)

16. **"Lei non è più qui?"** "No, lei è partita due **mesi fa."**

    "She's not <u>still</u> here?" "No, she left <u>two months ago."</u>

FIFTEEN.

HITHER, THITHER, AND YON: EXPRESSIONS OF PLACE

As with the last chapter, which dealt with expressions of time, this is a reference chapter. Here we will be dealing with expressions of place. Browse lightly through the chapter now, to get an idea of what it contains, but don't, unless you are really interested, try to memorize the material. Instead, come back when you are searching for an expression of place.

The entries will be listed first in English, then Italian, since English is probably the language you will be thinking in when you want to use one of the expressions. All of them will be shown in the context of a phrase or sentence.

The chapter is divided into four sections, to wit:

1. <u>Hither</u>: expressions of places that are, or could be, very near to you.

2. <u>Thither</u>: things or places that are probably within your line of sight or hearing.

3. <u>Yon</u>: things or places that are probably remote.

4. Names of places you might want to visit.

Obviously some of these artificial distinctions won't always work, but we will try to operate on the general principle of starting from <u>here</u> and going slowly to <u>there</u>.

HITHER

1. above

   Above us (upstairs) lives a little old lady.

   sopra

   Sopra di noi abita una vecchina.

2. around, near

   The boy is around (near) the pool.

   intorno a

   Il ragazzo è **intorno alla** piscina.

3. behind

   There is a big garden behind the house.

   dietro

   C'è un gran giardino **dietro** la casa.

4. below, under

   The cat sleeps under the table.

   sotto

   Il gatto dorme **sotto** la tavola.

5. close to, near

   Our house is close to yours.

   vicino a

   La nostra casa è **vicino alla** vostra.

6. down

   Come down from there!

   giù

   Vieni **giù** di là!

7. here

   The mail is here.

   qui, qua; ecco *

   La posta è **qui** (**qua**).
   Ecco la posta.

8. in (a building)

   Elena is in the church.

   in (sometimes + article)

   Elena è **in** chiesa.

9. in (a city)

   Pietro is in Florence.

   a

   Pietro è **a** Firenze.

10. in (a country)

    Carlo is in the United States.

    in + (article)

    Carlo è **negli** Stati Uniti.

---

* The term **ecco** in its many variations carries the meaning of a successful demonstration, as does the French **voilà**.
Thus on arriving at a place, you may hear "**Eccoci!**" -- "Here we are!" Did you ask for french fries? "**Eccole!**" -- "Here they are!"

11. in front of	The baptistery is <u>in front of</u> the cathedral.
davanti a	Il battistero è **davanti al** duomo.
12. inside (of)	The statue is <u>inside</u> the museum.
dentro	La statua è **dentro** il museo.
13. next to	John is <u>next to</u> Maria.
accanto a	Giovanni è **accanto a** Maria.
14. through	We met while walking <u>through</u> the city.
per	Ci siamo incontrati mentre camminavamo **per** la città.
15. up	The train goes <u>up</u> the mountain.
su	Il treno va **su** per la montagna.
16. up and down	These children are always going <u>up and down</u>.
su e giù	Questi bambini vanno sempre **su e giù**.

THITHER

17. at the back	The shoe department is <u>at the back</u> of the store.
in fondo	Il reparto calzatura è **in fondo** al negozio.
18. beyond, past	The station is 100 meters <u>beyond</u> the church.
al di là **passato, oltre**	La stazione è 100 metri **oltre** la chiesa.

An Italian Tonguetwister

The word for tonguetwister is **scioglilingua**, a "tongue untier." Try saying this one fast three times, even if it doesn't make too much sense:

Sopra la panca, la capra campa; **sotto** la panca, la capra crepa.

<u>On top of</u> the bench, the goat rests; <u>under</u> the bench, the goat bursts.

19.	few steps	The restaurant is a <u>few steps</u> from here.
	a due passi	Il ristorante è qui **a due passi.**
20.	halfway	The town is <u>halfway</u> between Florence and Rome.
	a metà (mezza) strada	Il paese è **a mezzastrada** fra Firenze e Roma.
21.	intersection	This is a dangerous <u>intersection</u>.
	incrocio	Questo è un **incrocio** pericoloso.
22.	meters	The building is 100 <u>meters</u> from here.
	metri	L'edificio è a 100 **metri** da qua.
23.	one-way	Via Antinori is a <u>one-way</u> street.
	senso unico	Via Antinori è una via a **senso unico.**
24.	out, outside	The cat is <u>out(side)</u>.
	fuori	Il gatto è **fuori.**
25.	stoplight	Turn right at the <u>stoplight</u>.
	semaforo	Gira a destra al **semaforo.**
26.	straight ahead	To find the fountain go <u>straight ahead</u>.
	sempre diritto	Per trovare la fontana, vai **sempre diritto.**
27.	street corner	Turn right at the <u>street corner</u>.
	angolo	Gira a destra all'**angolo.**
28.	there	The church is <u>there</u>.
	lì, * là *,	La chiesa è **lì** (**là**).
	ci	Let's go <u>there</u>!
		Andiamoci!

---

* A little rhyme should help you with your spelling:

L'accento non va con "qui" e "qua";
L'accento si fa con "lì" e "là."

No accent mark's used with "qui" and "qua";
It always goes with "lì" and "là."

29. to a building	Let's go <u>to</u> school, ... <u>to</u> the movies.
a	Andiamo **a** scuola, ... **al** cinema.
30. to a person	Let's go <u>to</u> Mary's, ... <u>to</u> the doctor.
da	Andiamo **da** Maria, ... **dal** dottore.
31. to a place	Let's go <u>to</u> the mountains, ... <u>to</u> the countryside.
in	Andiamo **in** montagna, ... **in** campagna.

Getting around in Italy is very easy. Anything indoors you want is **in fondo** and anything outdoors is **sempre diritto**. Virtually every time I've asked for directions in a department store, the clerks have assured me that what I want is **in fondo**, with a vague wave toward the back of the store. And a friend reports: "I always found directions sounded terribly similar and never very clear, no matter where I was going. Invariably I was supposed to go **sempre diritto**."

AND YON

A Geopolitical Note on Italy

Italy is a <u>state</u>, divided into several <u>regions</u>, just as we have a <u>federal government</u> divided into several <u>states</u>. When you read in Italian newspapers of a matter **dello stato**, a matter of the state, you are reading about something affecting the central government in Rome. Because we are so accustomed to associating the word "state" with one of the 50 United States, rather than the federal government, it takes a little getting used to in making the transition to the Italian political organization.

This having been said, note that the capital of the state government in Italy, **capitale** or **sede del governo statale d'Italia** is Rome, just as Washington, D.C. is for the United States. (Note that **sede** derives from the verb **sedere**, to sit, and that **sede** and <u>seat</u> are QC's.)

Mainland Italy is divided into 20 regions (**regioni**), equivalent to our states. Each of these regions and Italy's islands also has a chief place of government, **un capoluogo**, equivalent to our state capitals. Five well-known regions and their capitals are the following: **Toscana - Firenze** (Tuscany - Florence), **Lazio - Roma** (Latium - Rome), **Lombardia - Milano** (Lombardy - Milan), **Liguria - Genova**, (Liguria - Genoa), and **Piemonte - Torino** (Piedmont - Turin).

Within each of the regions are a number of provinces, **province**, roughly equivalent to American counties, each usually bearing the name of its major city. Alcune delle provincie di **Toscana**, per esempio, sono **Firenze, Siena, Livorno** (Leghorn), e **Pisa**. License plates -- **targhe** -- on cars identify the province of provenance by the first of its letters or a similar abbreviation. Cars from the cities just named would have license plates starting, respectively: **FI, SI, LI**, and **PI**. For instance, a car licensed **FI-3/8652** would be from the province of **FIrenze**. Cars from the province of Torino would start **TO**, those from Genova, **GE**, etc.

A <u>municipality</u> (city, town) is a **comune**; its boundaries or limits (or those of a province, region, or the country) are **i confini**.

When the word **Paese**, capitalized, is used, it usually refers to a country or nation, e.g. **Il Paese d'Italia**. When it is not capitalized, it suggests a little locality, e.g. **il piccolo paese di Sori, vicino a Genova** (the little town of Sori, near Genoa).

Much of the foregoing will be exemplified in the two following paragraphs:

Luigi was born in the town of Sori, a little village in the province of Genoa. Genoa is also the capital of its region, Liguria. Luigi grew up within the boundaries of the province and then drove a car licensed GE-5/4907 to visit the capital of his country, Rome.

Luigi è nato **nel comune** di Sori, **un piccolo paese in provincia** di Genova. Genova è anche **il capoluogo della sua regione**, la Liguria. Luigi è cresciuto **tra i confini della provincia** e poi ha guidato in una macchina **targata GE-5/4907** per visitare Roma, **la sede del governo del suo Paese**.

Some Geographic Terms

32. capital (of country) The <u>capital</u> (<u>seat of government</u>) of Italy is Rome.

    sede del governo, capitale La **capitale** (**sede del governo**) d'Italia è Roma.

33. city Milan is a most important <u>city</u>.

    città Milano è una **città** importantissima.

34. national borders I was born within the <u>national borders</u> of the United States.

    i confini Sono nato **tra i confini** degli Stati Uniti.

35. country, nation Italy is an historic <u>country</u> (<u>nation</u>).

    Paese L'Italia è un **Paese** storico.

36. hills There are many <u>hills</u> around Florence.

    colline Intorno a Firenze ci sono molte **colline**.

37. island Sicily is Italy's biggest <u>island</u>.

    isola La Sicilia è **l'isola** più grande d'Italia.

38. lake <u>Lake</u> Como is beautiful.

    lago Il **lago** di Como è bello.

39. river The Arno <u>river</u> passes through Florence.

    fiume Il **fiume** Arno passa per Firenze.

40. region Apulia is one of the <u>regions</u> of Italy.

    regione La Puglia è uno **delle regioni** d'Italia.

41. suburbs Arcetri is one of the <u>suburbs</u> of Florence.

    dintorni Arcetri è uno dei **dintorni** di Firenze.

42. small town, little place Sori is a <u>small town</u> near Genoa.

    piccolo paese Sori è un **piccolo paese** vicino a Genova.

Modes of Transportation. In English, if you want to get to one of these places, you go <u>by</u> a given mode of transportation, e.g. <u>by</u> car, <u>by</u> train, <u>by</u> boat, etc. In Italian, one usually goes <u>in</u>, as shown by these examples:

by bicycle	in bicicletta
by bus	in autobus
by car	in macchina
by plane	in aeroplano, in aereo
by train	in treno

The major exception to this is in saying <u>by foot</u>, or <u>on foot</u>, which in Italian is **a piedi**.

Local Places. The places listed in "Yon" have primarily been geographic places, often at some distance. Below find a list of places you might want to find in your own city.

the airport	l'aeroporto
the bakery	la pasticceria
the bar	il bar
the car rental	l'autonoleggio
the church	la chiesa
the downtown area	il centro
the food store	gli alimentari
the fountain	la fontana
the hotel	l'albergo
the ice cream shop	la gelateria
the jewelry shop	la gioielleria
the movie house	il cinema
the museum	il museo
the park	il parco
the pharmacy	la farmacia
the delicatessen *	la rosticceria *
the post office	l'ufficio postale
the restaurant	il ristorante, la trattoria
the square	la piazza
the train station	la stazione
the store	il negozio
the zoo	il giardino zoologico

---

* These are places where meats and poultry are often being cooked over the spit while cold cuts and salads are available at the counter. You can order your food "to go," or there may be a back room where you can sit and eat.

QUIZ ON EXPRESSIONS OF PLACE

As with the quiz on expressions of time, you can defer this one until you have started using these expressions of place, unless you would like to venture forth now to use the quiz as a spur to learning.

Translate the sentences into the other language; key words are emphasized in both the quiz and the answers on the following pages.

1. Let's go <u>downtown</u> today to shop.

_____

2. I am going <u>to Florence</u> this summer.

_____

3. He is going <u>to the country</u> to find the <u>little villages</u>.

_____

4. When you come to <u>the intersection</u>, <u>turn left</u> and then continue <u>straight ahead</u>.

_____

5. The dog sleeps <u>under</u> the table.

_____

6. Marco went <u>to the doctor</u> and then <u>to the pharmacy</u>.

_____

7. They are <u>taking a walk</u> <u>through the park</u>.

_____

8. The church is over <u>there</u>, <u>next to</u> the fountain.

_____

9. La famiglia è andata **al cinema in macchina.**

_____

10. **Eccoci!** Adesso, andiamo **a scuola.**

_____

11. Il ristorante è **lungo il fiume.**

_____

12. Quella chiesa è **fuori del comune.**

_____

13. La macchina ha **girato a destra verso il senso unico.**

_____

14. La statua di Davide è **dentro il museo.**

_____

15. Firenze è **vicina al piccolo paese** di Fiesole.

_____

16. Questa strada va sempre **su e giù.**

_____

Answers to Quiz on Expressions of Place

1. Let's go <u>downtown</u> today to shop.

   Andiamo **in centro** oggi per fare le spese.

2. I am going <u>to Florence</u> this summer.

   Vado **a Firenze** quest'estate.

3. He is going <u>to the country</u> to find the <u>little villages</u>.

   Va **in campagna** per trovare **i piccoli paesi.**

4. When you come to <u>the intersection,</u> <u>turn left</u> and then continue <u>straight ahead</u>.

   Quando arrivi **all'incrocio, gira a sinistra,** e poi continua **sempre diritto.**

5. The dog sleeps <u>under</u> the table.

   Il cane dorme **sotto** la tavola.

6. Marco went <u>to the doctor</u> and then <u>to the pharmacy</u>.

   Marco è andato **dal dottore** e poi **in farmacia.**

7. They are <u>taking a walk through the park</u>.

   Fanno **quattro passi (una passegiata) nel parco.**

8. The church is over <u>there</u>, <u>next to</u> the fountain.

   La chiesa è **là, accanto alla** fontana.

9. La famiglia è andata **al cinema in macchina.**

   The family went <u>to the movie by car</u>.

10. **Eccoci!** Adesso, andiamo **a scuola.**

    <u>Here we are!</u> Let's go <u>to school</u> now.

11. Il ristorante è **lungo il fiume.**

    The restaurant is <u>along</u> (<u>by</u>) the river.

12. Quella chiesa è **fuori del comune.**

    That church is <u>outside of the city</u>.

13. La macchina ha **girato a destra verso il senso unico.**

    The car <u>turned right onto a one-way street</u>.

14. La statua di Davide è **dentro il museo.**

    The statue of David is <u>inside the museum</u>.

15. Firenze è **vicina al piccolo paese** di Fiesole.

    Florence is <u>near the little town</u> of Fiesole.

16. Questa strada va sempre **su e giù.**

    This street keeps going <u>up and down</u>.

SIXTEEN.

MORE COGNATES UNFAITHFUL AND QUASI

Again we are about to pick up on tasks started in earlier chapters. The first is to continue listing Unfaithful Cognates (UC), words that resemble each other in spelling and pronunciation, but have quite different meanings in the two languages.

Then we will list some more Quasi-Cognates (QC), words with a modest resemblance to each other and quite similar meanings.

Quizzes will appear as usual.

MORE UNFAITHFUL COGNATES

controllare   Used much more in the sense of to inspect or check, as in "un **controllo** del passaporto" (a passport <u>check</u> at customs) than of to direct someone's actions (which usually is **dirigere**) or to govern (which is **govenare**).

diplomato   A person who holds a diploma, <u>not</u> a diplomat in the political sense (who is a **diplomatico**).

drogheria	A general store, <u>not</u> a drugstore-pharmacy (which is **farmacia**).
educazione	**Educazione** means upbringing, good breeding; someone who is **maleducato** is someone with poor manners and breeding. (See also **istruzione.**)
effettivo	Actual, real, current, <u>not</u> effective (which is **efficace** or **in vigore**).
eventualmente	If, in case, but <u>not</u> eventually, something that will finally occur (which is **finalmente** or **alla fine**).
fabbrica	A factory, <u>not</u> a farm (which is **fattoria**).
fattoria	A farm, <u>not</u> a factory (which is **fabbrica**).
geniale	Ingenious, clever, <u>not</u> genial or cordial (which is **cordiale**).
ginnasio	A secondary school, <u>not</u> a gymnasium (which is **palestra**).
istruzione	**Istruzione** means instruction or education, e.g. **istruzione tecnica** is <u>technical education</u>.
largo	Wide, <u>not</u> large (which is **grande**).
magazzino	Large store or storage area, <u>not</u> a published magazine (which is **rivista**).
morbido	Soft, delicate, <u>not</u> morbid or unhealthy (which is **morboso**).
morboso	Morbid or unhealthy, <u>not</u> soft, delicate (which is **morbido**).
negozio	A shop or store, <u>not</u> negotiation (which is **trattativa**).
omaggio	A complimentary gift (used more frequently in this sense than that of <u>homage</u>, though that is proper usage, too).
opportunità	An opportunity to be seized upon (distinct connotations of opportunism), only rarely as an innocent chance or possibility of doing something (which is **avere la possibilità**).
registrare	To record, as on tape (such a tape is **un nastro di registrazione**), or to record a birth; <u>not</u> to be confused with **ricordare** (which is <u>to remember</u>).

ricordar(si)   To remember (**un ricordo** is a souvenir), <u>not</u> to
                 record a tape or a birth (which is **registrare**).

sensibile   Notable, can be sensed or touched, <u>not</u> sensible,
                 reasonable (which is **ragionevole**).

Quiz on More Unfaithful Cognates

Translate the following sentences into the other language,
being especially careful with the emphasized words or phrases.

1. The gas station attendant <u>has inspected</u> the oil.

   _____

2. He is a <u>sensible</u> (<u>reasonable</u>) person.

   _____

3. The doctor will call the <u>drugstore</u>.

   _____

4. She is a very <u>clever</u> (<u>ingenious</u>) person.

   _____

5. These matches were made in a <u>factory</u>.

   _____

6. He lived on a <u>farm</u>.

   _____

7. This medicine is <u>effective</u>.

   _____

8. I would like <u>to have an opportunity</u> to travel.

   _____

9. Lui ha avuto una buona **educazione**.

_____

10. Si può comprare il sapone alla **drogheria**.

_____

11. Questa stoffa (cloth) è **morbida**.

_____

12. Ho trovato la macchina per scrivere nel **magazzino**.

_____

13. Lui l'ha letto nella **rivista**.

_____

14. Questa carta geografica è data **in omaggio** dall'Autoclub.

_____

15. Lui è un **diplomatico** che fa **trattative** per il suo paese.

_____

16. Lei frequenta un **ginnasio**.

_____

Answers to Quiz on More Unfaithful Cognates

1. The gas station attendant <u>has inspected</u> the oil.

   Il benzinaio **ha controllato** l'olio.

2. He is a <u>sensible</u> (<u>reasonable</u>) person.

   Lui è una persona **ragionevole**.

3. The doctor will call the <u>drugstore</u>.

   Il medico telefonerà alla **farmacia**.

4. She is a very <u>clever</u> (<u>ingenious</u>) person.

   Lei è una persona molto **geniale**.

5. These matches were made in a <u>factory</u>.

   Questi fiammiferi sono stati fatti in una **fabbrica**.

6. He lived on a <u>farm</u>.

   Abitava in una **fattoria**.

7. This medicine is <u>effective</u>.

   Questa medicina è **efficace**.

8. I would like <u>to have an opportunity</u> to travel.

   Vorrei **avere la possibilità** di viaggiare.

9. Lui ha avuto una buona **educazione**.

    He has had a good upbringing.

10. Si può comprare il sapone in **drogheria**.

    One can buy the soap at the general store.

11. Questa stoffa (cloth) è **morbida**.

    This cloth is soft.

12. Ho trovato la macchina per scrivere nel **magazzino**.

    I found the typewriter in the storage room (or large store).

13. Lui l'ha letto nella **rivista**.

    He read it in a magazine.

14. Questa carta geografica è data **in omaggio** dall'Autoclub.

    This map is given as a complimentary copy by the Autoclub.

15. Lui è un **diplomatico** che fa **trattative** per il suo paese.

    He is a diplomat who negotiates for his country.

16. Lei frequenta un **ginnasio**.

    She goes to (attends) a secondary school.

A Last Batch of Unfaithful Cognates

Here's a last batch of Unfaithful Cognates; no quiz this time. Individual UC's will continue to be identified in other chapters when they appear.

alunno   Student, <u>not</u> alumnus (which is **ex-allievo**).

avviso   Notice, as in **Avviso Importante** (<u>Important Notice</u>), <u>not</u> advice (which is **consiglio**, of which <u>counsel</u> is a QC).

camera   A room, as in an apartment or hotel, <u>not</u> a photo camera (which is **macchina fotografica**).

carattere   Personality, disposition, <u>not</u> character as of a person (which is **personaggio**).

fornitura   A supply, <u>not</u> furniture (which is/are **mobili**, plural in Italian).

graduare   To scale, make a graduated scale; **gradi** are degrees of temperature, for instance; <u>not</u> to graduate from school (which is **laurearsi**).

idioma   Language, <u>not</u> idiom as in idiomatic expression (which is **espressione idiomatica**).

novella   A short story (which can be long), but <u>not</u> a full-blown novel (which is **romanzo**).

storia   Usually history, usually <u>not</u> a story or anecdote (which is **racconto**, and one who tells a good story is a "raconteur").

QUASI-COGNATES

Below we will list three groups of Quasi-Cognates, with 20 pairs in each group. Each group is followed by a quiz. Memorize as many of the groups now as you feel like; leave the remainder to come back to when the mood seizes you.

Group A of More Quasi-Cognates

to bar	sbarrare
the change	il cambio
the day	il dì
the development	lo sviluppo
to diminish	diminuire

the discontent	lo scontento
the discount	lo sconto
the encounter	l'incontro
the engineer	l'ingegnere
to fascinate	affascinare

incendiary	accendere (to light)
isolation	isolamento
mad (insane)	matto
poor, poverty	povero, povertà
to revolve	volgere

sand	sabbia
to seek, search	cercare
the square	quadrato
street	la strada
the table	la tavola

Quiz on Group A of More Quasi-Cognates

Supply the missing words.

the development _____

the sand _____

the discontent _____

the change _____

the street _____

the table _____

poor (adj.) _____

the isolation _____

the encounter _____

to fascinate _____

_____ matto

_____ diminuire

_____ cercare

_____ sbarrare

_____ accendere

_____ quadrato

_____ ingegnere

_____ dì

_____ lo sconto

_____ volgere

the development	lo sviluppo
the sand	la sabbia
the discontent	lo scontento
the change	il cambio
the street	la strada

the table	la tavola
poor (adj.)	povero
the isolation	l'isolamento
the encounter	l'incontro
to fascinate	affascinare

mad (insane)	matto
to diminish	diminuire
to seek, search	cercare
to bar	sbarrare
incendiary	accendere

square	quadrato
engineer	ingegnere
the day	dì
the discount	lo sconto
to revolve	volgere

Group B of More Quasi-Cognates

Here we go again. Do as you did for Group A.

to collect	cogliere
to cook	cucinare
the delusion	il delirio
to discharge	scaricare
the disdain	sdegno

to doubt	dubitare
the effort	lo sforzo
to evaluate	valutare
the fact	il fatto
the isle	l'isola

the law	la legge
the number	il numero
the reason	la ragione
rough	rozzo
speedy	spedito

to suck	succhiare
to summarize	riassumere
sure, secure	sicuro
surgery	chirurgia
to terrify	terrorizzare

the disdain   _____

the effort   _____

to doubt   _____

the number   _____

to suck   _____

to collect   _____

to evaluate   _____

the delusion   _____

to cook   _____

the fact   _____

_____   la ragione

_____   terrorizzare

_____   riassumere

_____   scaricare

_____   l'isola

_____   sicuro

_____   spedito

_____   rozzo

_____   chirurgia

_____   la legge

Answers to Quiz on Group B

the disdain	lo sdegno
the effort	lo sforzo
to doubt	dubitare
the number	il numero
to suck	succhiare

to collect	cogliere
to evaluate	valutare
the delusion	il delirio
to cook	cucinare
the fact	il fatto

the reason	la ragione
to terrify	terrorizzare
to summarize	riassumere
to discharge	scaricare
the isle	l'isola

sure, secure	sicuro
speedy	spedito
rough	rozzo
surgery	chirurgia
the law	la legge

to commence (begin)	cominciare
to counsel (advise)	consigliare
debilitated (weak)	debole
to explain	spiegare
the flame	la fiamma
to gain (earn)	guadagnare
the justice	la giustizia
to obey	obbedire
the plant	la pianta
the proof (trial)	la prova
the party (political)	il partito
to roast	arrostire
round, rotund	rotondo
satisfied	soddisfatto
to select	scegliere
the soap	il sapone
the sign	il segno
to spit	sputare
the spite	il dispetto
useful, utilizable	utile

Quiz on Group C of More Quasi-Cognates

to spit   _____

to gain   _____

satisfied   _____

the justice   _____

to counsel (advise)   _____

the sign   _____

to roast   _____

weak (debilitated)   _____

the spite   _____

to select   _____

_____   la prova

_____   la fiamma

_____   cominciare

_____   la pianta

_____   il sapone

_____   il partito

_____   spiegare

_____   obbedire

_____   utile

_____   rotondo

to spit	sputare
to gain	guadagnare
satisfied	soddisfatto
the justice	la giustizia
to counsel (advise)	consigliare
the sign	il segno
to roast	arrostire
debilitated (weak)	debole
the spite	il dispetto
to select	scegliere
the proof (trial)	la prova
the flame	la fiamma
to commence, begin	cominciare
the plant	la pianta
the soap	il sapone
the party (political)	il partito
to explain	spiegare
to obey	obbedire
useful, utilizable	utile
round, rotund	rotondo

SEVENTEEN.

MORE POPULAR ITALIAN WORDS AND PHRASES

The words and phrases given in our previous chapter on this topic were those commonly found in speech, newspapers, and on television. We will continue them below.

There is another category of words and phrases that often serve as much as verbal punctuation of conversations as they convey specific information; they will be listed in the second part of this chapter as "Interjections, Expostulations, and Ejaculations."

POPULAR WORDS AND PHRASES

1. **affatto**   Non posso sopportarti **affatto!**

   at all   I can't stand you <u>at all!</u>

2. **al dente**   Queste fettucine sono **al dente.**

   firm (of pasta)   These noodles are <u>firm</u>.

3. **avercela**

Non voglio sentirti più. **C'è l'ho** fin qua!

to have had it with
someone, something

I don't want to listen to you anymore.
<u>I've had it</u> up to here!

4. **avere l'acqua
in bocca**

Queste parole sono segrete; ricordati --
acqua in bocca!

don't breathe
a word

These words are secret; remember --
<u>don't breathe a word</u>.

5. **cin cin**

Cin cin a tutti i laureati!

cheers; bottoms up
(drinking toast)

<u>Cheers</u> to all the graduates!

6. **come al solito**

Hai fatto un buon compito, **come al solito.**

as usual

You've done a nice job, <u>as usual</u>.

7. **dica; mi dica**

Mi dica, signora, cosa desidera?

speak; tell me
(polite form)

<u>Tell me</u>, ma'am, what would you like?

8. **esser pieno di sè**

Quel mio cugino è sempre **pieno di sè.**

to be full of
one's self

That cousin of mine is <u>always</u>
<u>full of himself</u>.

9. **faccia pure!**

"Potrei guardare queste ceramiche?"
"Sì, **faccia pure!**"

please, do as you
wish

"May I look at these ceramics?"
"Of course, <u>do as you wish</u>!"

10. **fare una
bella figura**

Maria fa sempre **una bella figura**
con i suoi vestiti.

to make a good
impression

Maria always <u>makes a good impression</u>
(cuts a fine <u>figure</u>) with her clothes.

11. **figurati!**

"Grazie per l'uso della macchina."
"**Figurati!**"

don't mention it!

"Thanks for the use of the car."
"<u>Don't mention it!</u>"

12. **forza!**

Forza Fiorentina! **Forza** ragazzi!

onward; charge;
let's get going!

<u>Go</u> Florentines! Come on kids,
<u>let's get going</u>!

13. **in bocca al lupo**   In bocca al lupo con l'esame domani.

    good luck (lit.   <u>Good luck</u> with the exam tomorrow.
    "in the mouth of
    the wolf")

    che crepi   (response to **in bocca al lupo**)

    let the wolf die   (Failure to respond means bad luck.)

14. **lo spiritoso**   Non fare **lo spiritoso**.

    smart aleck   Don't be a <u>smart aleck</u>.

15. **meno male**   Piove? **Meno male** che c'è un bel film alla TV.

    just as well   It's raining? It's <u>just as well</u> that
                          there's a good film on TV.

16. **neanche per sogno**   Io -- ballare con te? **Neanche per sogno!**

    not on your life   Me -- dance with you? <u>Not on your life</u>!

17. **non fa niente**   "Mi scusi, signore." "**Non fa niente.**"

    it's nothing;   "Excuse me, sir." "<u>It's nothing (it</u>
    not important   <u>doesn't matter)</u>."

18. **non fare**   Se hai ancora fame, mangia pure, senza **fare**
    complimenti   **complimenti**.

    don't be shy   If you're still hungry, go ahead and eat;
    (out of courtesy)   <u>don't be shy</u>.

19. **pasticcio;**   Che **pasticcio** hai combinato!
    che pasticcio

    a mess; what a mess   <u>What a mess</u> you've made!

20. **proprio**   Tu sei stato **proprio** al Palio?

    really; exactly   Were you <u>really</u> at the Palio?

21. **punto e basta**   Gianni è un cretino! **Punto e basta!**

    that's it, period!   Gianni is an idiot! <u>That's it, period</u>!

22. **senz'altro**

Puoi venire a casa mia stasera? **Senz'altro.**

but of course;
without a doubt

Can you come to my house tonight? <u>Sure,
without a doubt</u>.

23. **stanco morto**

Dopo quel viaggio di sedici ore, sono
stanco morto.

dead tired

After that 16-hour trip, I'm <u>dead tired</u>.

24. **toccare a**

Questa volta **tocca a** me pagare la birra

to be one's turn

This time it's <u>my turn</u> to pay for the beer.

INTERJECTIONS, EXPOSTULATIONS, AND EJACULATIONS

Certain words and phrases serve as much as punctuation for speech as for relaying specific information. Sometimes they serve as "filler words," allowing the speaker to pause to collect a mental breath before proceeding. All the words and phrases listed below have a specific and legitimate meaning, but often they are used as punctuation. If you hear the word or phrase and it doesn't seem to fit in context, remember that the speaker might just as well be clearing his/her throat.

25. **ad ogni modo**

Ad ogni modo, fa' come tu credi meglio.

in any case

<u>In any case</u>, do as you think best.

26. **allora**

Allora, volete venire con noi o no?

then; well then

<u>Well then</u>, do you want to come
with us or not?

27. **altro che!**

Io ci andrei in Italia? **Altro che!**

of course!;
you betcha!

Me go to Italy? <u>You betcha</u>!

28. **be'** (abbrev.
of 'bene')

Be', se proprio non vuoi venire ...

well

<u>Well</u>, if you really don't want to come ...

29. **bo!; boh!**
(said with shrug)

Gianni non è ancora venuto? **Boh!**

So? Well? Who knows?

Isn't Gianni here yet? <u>Who knows</u>?

30. **cioè**

    that is

Vorrei spiegare questo, **cioè**,
renderlo più chiaro.

I would like to explain this, <u>that is</u>,
make it clearer.

31. **comunque**

    however

Io ho dato dei suggerimenti; **comunque**,
fate pure.

I've made some suggestions; <u>however</u>, do
as you please.

32. **da'!; dai!**

    (from **dare**)
    give! tell me!

Chi è il suo nuovo ragazzo? **Dai!**

Who's her new boyfriend? <u>Tell me!</u>

33. **davvero!**

    really?! in truth!

L'Italia ha appena vinto la coppa
mondiale. **Davvero?!**

Italy just won the world cup. <u>Really</u>?!

34. **dunque**

    well then;
    therefore;
    let's see

Dunque, se mi ricordo bene ...

<u>Let's see</u>, if I remember correctly ...

35. **ecco**

    here; here it is;
    here we are
    (agreement)

(1) **Ecco** i soldi che ti devo.
(2) **Eccoci!** (3) **Ecco**, sono d'accordo.

(1) <u>Here is</u> the money I owe you.
(2) <u>Here we are</u>. (3) <u>Yes</u>, I agree.

36. **eh, già**

    ah, yes

Eh, già, figlio mio, la vita è dura.

<u>Ah yes</u>, my son, life is tough.

37. **fregarsene**

    to not give a damn;
    to not care

Francamente, mia cara, **non me ne frega!**

Frankly, my dear, <u>I don't give a damn!</u>

38. **infatti**

    in fact; as a
    matter of fact

Infatti, non è una cosa che
tocca a lui fare.

<u>In fact</u>, it's not something that's
up to him to do.

39. **insomma**

in sum; well then;
in conclusion

Insomma, tutto quello che ti ho
detto è vero.

<u>Well then</u> (after all), everything I've told
you is true.

40. **perciò**

so; therefore

Ho trovato un taxi, **perciò** sono
arrivato presto.

I found a taxi, <u>so</u> I arrived early.

41. **però**

but; however

Di solito vengo volentieri, **però**
oggi mi sento un po' male.

Usually I would be glad to come, <u>but</u>
today I feel a little off.

42. **poi**

then

Abbiamo deciso, **poi**, di andare al cinema.

We've decided, <u>then</u>, to go to the movies.

43. **quindi**

so; therefore

Quindi, perchè non venite domani sera?

<u>So</u>, why don't you come tomorrow night?

44. **sai?**
(from 'sapere')

you know?
(said with rising
inflection)

Domani viene Luigi, lo **sai**?

Luigi comes tomorrow, <u>you know</u>?

45. **via**

come on

Via, non dire così!

<u>Come on</u>, don't talk that way!

EIGHTEEN.

FOR AN IRREGULAR PASSATO REMOTO, DIAL 133.212

PROFESSOR ORVIETO'S MAGIC NUMBER

In the summer of 1981, Professor Orvieto of the Università per Stranieri in Perugia presented us with a **trucco** (trick) to help remember how to form the **passato remoto** for irregular verbs. The **trucco** consisted primarily in learning his magic number, namely:

133.212

We will not deal here with forming the **passato remoto** for regular verbs; that consists of simple and straightforward memorization of the requisite endings. Instead we will deal only with the irregulars. What you need to know, to use the magic number, is (1) the infinitive, and (2) the irregular form in the first person singular, e.g.: **leggere - lessi, conoscere - conobbi, correre - corsi,** etc.

HOW TO USE THE MAGIC NUMBER

Inspect this table for **legg**/ere - **less**/i

Person	Irregular Stem	Infinitive Stem

Singular

(1) First	**less**/i	
(2) Second		**legg**/esti
(3) Third	**less**/e	

Plural

(1) First		**legg**/emmo
(2) Second		**legg**/este
(3) Third	**less**/ero	

The first three digits of magic number -- 133 -- refer to the first-person singular, third-person singular, third-person plural. The second three digits -- 212 -- refer to the second-person singular, first-person plural, second-person plural. In tabular form it looks like this:

Number	Reference	Example
1	First (sing.)	**less**/i
3	Third (sing.)	**less**/e
3	Third (plural)	**less**/ero
. . . . .	. . . .	. . . .
2	Second (sing.)	**legg**/esti
1	First (plural)	**legg**/emmo
2	Second (plural)	**legg**/este

The 133 forms come from the irregular past form, **less**/-. The 212 forms are based on the infinitive, **legg**/-. That's the crux of it, friends: For these verbs, use the irregular stem for the 133 forms and the infinitive for the 212 forms.

Once you have this notion firmly in mind, it is only necessary to memorize the endings that attach to one or the other stem, as shown in the example. To help nail it down, here is the **passato remoto** for **conosc**/ere - **conobb**/i.

	Person	Irregular Stem	Infinitive Stem

Person	Irregular Stem	Infinitive Stem

Singular

Person		Irregular Stem	Infinitive Stem
(1)	First	conobb/i	
(2)	Second		conosc/esti
(3)	Third	conobb/e	

Plural

Person		Irregular Stem	Infinitive Stem
(1)	First		conosc/emmo
(2)	Second		conosc/este
(3)	Third	conobb/ero	

PRACTICE MAKES PERFECT: AN EXERCISE

Using the examples of **leggere - lessi** and **conoscere - conobbi** as models (peeking at them is not only fair, it is encouraged), fill in the blanks below for **correre** and **volere**. As you will note, there are 12 blanks for each verb, but only six of them will be filled in, so probably you should first put an "x" at the beginning of a blank where you know you will be making an entry and then leave the blank blanks blank. Then go ahead and put in, first, the stems, and then the endings that attach to the stems. Check against the answers on the following page.

Person	Irregular Stem	Infinitive Stem	Irregular Stem	Infinitive Stem
correre - corsi			**volere - volli**	

Singular

Person	Irregular Stem	Infinitive Stem	Irregular Stem	Infinitive Stem
First	_____	_____	_____	_____
Second	_____	_____	_____	_____
Third	_____	_____	_____	_____

Plural

Person	Irregular Stem	Infinitive Stem	Irregular Stem	Infinitive Stem
First	_____	_____	_____	_____
Second	_____	_____	_____	_____
Third	_____	_____	_____	_____

Answers to the Exercise

Person	Irregular Stem	Infinitive Stem	Irregular Stem	Infinitive Stem
correre – corsi			**volere – volli**	
Singular				
First	**cors**/i	_____	**voll**/i	_____
Second	_____	**corr**/esti	_____	**vol**/esti
Third	**cors**/e	_____	**voll**/e	_____
Plural				
First	_____	**corr**/emmo	_____	**vol**/emmo
Second	_____	**corr**/este	_____	**vol**/este
Third	**cors**/ero	_____	**voll**/ero	_____

And that's all there is to it. If you would like to try out a few more, be sure you have a copy of 201 Italian Verbs (by Luciani) at hand. Select your favorites from the list I'm about to give, write out the **passato remoto** for each, and then check against the "Past Absolute" listings in Luciani's book. Take your pick from these:

accendere – accesi	porre – posi
apprendere – appresi	ridere – risi
discutere – discussi	scrivere – scrissi
giungere – giunsi	tenere – tenni
mettere – misi	volgere – volsi

Bonus problem: Form the **passato remoto** for **fare – feci** and **dire – dissi**. These are tricky, because the 212 forms are based on their Latin (not their Italian) infinitives, which are **facere** and **dicere**, respectively. Figure it out on a piece of scratch paper first, then check against the answers on the bottom of this page.

---

fare (facere) – feci

Singular	Plural
feci	facemmo
facesti	faceste
fece	fecero

dire (dicere) – dissi

Singular	Plural
dissi	dicemmo
dicesti	diceste
disse	dissero

NINETEEN.

THE SUBJUNCTIVE (WITH FLOWCHARTS)

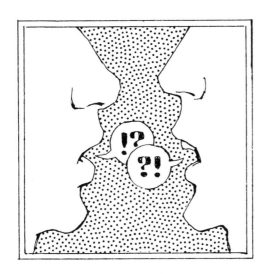

INTRODUCTION

This is the longest chapter in the book. Its length reflects the complexity of understanding and using the subjunctive (**congiuntivo**) in Italian. Though we have a subjunctive in English, its use is not nearly as widespread as it is in Italian, and thus we have to go to greater lengths to lay some groundwork before providing opportunities to use it.

The chapter is divided into three sections. The first section, "What the Subjunctive Is and How to Form It," describes the subjunctive and then provides tables showing the verb forms and endings for the four tenses of the subjunctive for the different conjugations. The tables come early in the chapter so you can get a feel for what the subjunctive looks like, <u>not</u> for you to memorize verb forms. The tables are a reference section to which you will be coming back later, when you are starting to translate sentences into the subjunctive.

The second section, "When to Use the Subjunctive," describes the eight major situations in which the subjunctive is called for, and it ends with a quiz to test your feel for identifying such situations.

The third section, "The Flowcharts," first describes four points at which you need to make a "Yes or No" decision about a sentence in which using the subjunctive is probably called for. Then it provides a series of decision-tree flowcharts that guide you to the proper verb form to use as you make your decisions. After the flowcharts, there are two quizzes in which you will be asked to translate English sentences into Italian. As you are taking the quizzes, you will be referring back to the tables to look up the verb forms you need. Answers to the quizzes will cite both the situation calling for the subjunctive (or sometimes the conditional) and the flowchart that directs you to the proper verb form.

It is the flowcharts that make this chapter unique. If you like flowcharts, you will love this chapter. Even if you don't like them, they should save you considerable grief, because they help you sort out the initially bewildering sets of rules for sequencing of tenses, forms, considerations of simultaneity, etc., which at first make the **congiuntivo** seem so confusing.

Even after you have mastered the material in this chapter, you will later learn that there are exceptions to the rules, that the rules apply perhaps 80% of the time. The foundation you build here will make the later learning of those exceptions and the reasons for them much easier.

Start reading Sections I and II now, not with the aim of memorizing what is in them, but more to familiarize yourself with their contents.* Then, when you start forming subjunctives in Section III, you will know where to look things up in the first two sections to be sure you are on the right track.

---

* Much of the information in the first two sections of this chapter, especially the material in Section II on when to use the subjunctive, is taken directly and with permission from materials presented by Joan Mammarella McConnell, Ph.D., at Stanford-in-Italy during the 1975-76 academic year.

Section I. What the Subjunctive Is and How to Form It

WHAT THE SUBJUNCTIVE IS

In Italian, the subjunctive, **congiuntivo**, could almost be called the "subjective." It is the mood of emotion, hope, doubt, fear, mystery. It is the mood of thinking, believing, wondering, speculating. The indicative states that which is <u>known</u>; the subjunctive tells us what <u>might be</u>. The subjunctive opens the window to the landscapes of the imagination.

We use the subjunctive less often in English, and if we are strict in following its forms, it sometimes sounds archaic or quaint, e.g. "If this be true," "If I were king," "Would that this were so," etc. The Italians, on the other hand, use the subjunctive much more extensively. Indeed, using it well is a sign of being well educated. And even if an American makes mistakes when trying to use the **congiuntivo**, the fact that you are trying at all will bring you both respect and sympathy from your Italian friends: respect for your bravery and sympathy because it was tough for them to learn it, too. (That's because they didn't have flowcharts!)

HOW TO FORM THE **CONGIUNTIVO**

The **congiuntivo** comes in four forms: present, imperfect, past, and pluperfect. These forms are shown in Table 19.1. Look the table over now, but promise you won't try to memorize anything. Just see what subjunctive forms look like.

In standard grammars and here, you will note that most examples using the **congiuntivo** are in the form:

    ... **che** + (pronoun) + (verb); e.g. ... **che tu AVESSI** *
    ... <u>that</u> + (pronoun) + (verb); e.g. ... <u>that you have</u>

In Italian, the **che** (<u>that</u>) is always used; in English it is sometimes optional.

             Penso **che** lui SIA ricco.
I think <u>that</u> he is rich. I think he is rich.

---

    * In this chapter, forms of the **congiuntivo** used in examples will be shown in CAPITAL LETTERS.

Note also that this is one instance in which one <u>must</u> use the pronoun in the singular in Italian to avoid ambiguity, even though the usage is optional in other moods because the verb endings already indicate which person is being used. Compare, for instance, the indicative and present subjunctive for **essere**:

<u>Indicative</u>	<u>Subjunctive</u>
sono	sia
sei	sia
è	sia
siamo	siamo
siete	siate
sono	siano

Thus our sentence above without the pronoun would read:

Penso **che** SIA ricco.

The SIA doesn't tell us whether the subject is second- or third-person; we don't know whether the rich person is you or he or she. So use the pronoun to be clear. (If the subject in both clauses had been the same, we would have used the <u>infinitive</u>, not the subjunctive -- all to be explained later.)

TABLE 19.1. THE SUBJUNCTIVE

THE PRESENT SUBJUNCTIVE

For Regular Verbs

parlare	**credere**	**dormire**
parli	creda	dorma
parli	creda	dorma
parli	creda	dorma
parliamo	crediamo	dormiamo
parliate	crediate	dormiate
parlino	credano	dormano

For Irregular Verbs

essere	**avere**	**tenere**	**capire**
sia	abbia	tenga	capisca
sia	abbia	tenga	capisca
sia	abbia	tenga	capisca
siamo	abbiamo	teniamo	capiamo
siate	abbiate	teniate	capiate
siano	abbiano	tengano	capiscano

N.B. In all forms, the first-person plural is the same as the indicative. In all second-person plurals, the letters -ia- occur, where only a single **a**, **e**, or **i** appeared in the indicative. In the third-person plurals, the vowel of the ending changes, e.g. **parlano - parlino**, etc.

Irregularities in the indicative are alive and well in the present subjunctive! The intrusive "g" of **tenere** and the -isc-stem of **capire** reign triumphant in all three singular forms and the third-person plural. Thus it will be for all verbs irregular in the present, something worth remembering.

TABLE 19.1. THE SUBJUNCTIVE (continued)

THE IMPERFECT SUBJUNCTIVE

For Regular Verbs

parlare	**credere**	**dormire**
parl/assi	cred/essi	dorm/issi
parl/assi	cred/essi	dorm/issi
parl/asse	cred/esse	dorm/isse
parl/assimo	cred/essimo	dorm/issimo
parl/aste	cred/este	dorm/iste
parl/assero	cred/essero	dorm/issero

For Irregular Verbs

essere	**avere**	**tenere**	**capire**
fossi	avessi	ten/essi	cap/issi
fossi	avessi	ten/essi	cap/issi
fosse	avesse	ten/esse	cap/isse
fossimo	avessimo	ten/essimo	cap/issimo
foste	aveste	ten/este	cap/iste
fossero	avessero	ten/essero	cap/issero

N.B. No irregularities appear (except for **essere**, but that's no surprise). In each case, the stem of the infinitive (including the vowels "a," "e," and "i" for the three conjugations) is followed by a regular set of endings identical for all. The irregularities of **tenere** (the intrusive "g") and **capire** (the -isc- stem) have disappeared entirely. Likewise do all such irregularities in the present indicative vanish in the imperfect subjunctive. **Grazie a Dio.**

TABLE 19.1. THE SUBJUNCTIVE (continued)

THE PAST SUBJUNCTIVE

For Regular Verbs

parlare	**credere**	**dormire**	**entrare**
abbia parlato	abbia creduto	abbia dormito	sia entrato(a)
abbia parlato	abbia creduto	abbia dormito	sia entrato(a)
abbia parlato	abbia creduto	abbia dormito	sia entrato(a)
abbiamo parlato	abbiamo creduto	abbiamo dormito	siamo entrati(e)
abbiate parlato	abbiate creduto	abbiate dormito	siate entrati(e)
abbiano parlato	abbiano creduto	abbiano dormito	siano entrati(e)

For Irregular Verbs

essere	**avere**	**tenere**	**capire**
sia stato(a)	abbia avuto	abbia tenuto	abbia capito
sia stato(a)	abbia avuto	abbia tenuto	abbia capito
sia stato(a)	abbia avuto	abbia tenuto	abbia capito
siamo stati(e)	abbiamo avuto	abbiamo tenuto	abbiamo capito
siate stati(e)	abbiate avuto	abbiate tenuto	abbiate capito
siano stati(e)	abbiano avuto	abbiano tenuto	abbiano capito

N.B. How very easy! It's just like the **passato prossimo** in the indicative, except that one uses the present **congiuntivo** of the verbs **essere** or **avere** with the past participle. The choice of which to use is exactly the same as in the indicative, so that in this table **essere** is used with **essere** and the verb of motion, **entrare**, and their participles reflect gender and number, as usual; otherwise it's **avere** all the way.

TABLE 19.1. THE SUBJUNCTIVE (continued)

THE PLUPERFECT SUBJUNCTIVE

For Regular Verbs

parlare	credere	dormire	entrare
avessi parlato	avessi creduto	avessi dormito	fossi entrato(a)
avessi parlato	avessi creduto	avessi dormito	fossi entrato(a)
avesse parlato	avesse creduto	avesse dormito	fosse entrato(a)
avessimo parlato	avessimo creduto	avessimo dormito	fossimo entrati(e)
aveste parlato	aveste creduto	aveste dormito	foste entrati(e)
avessero parlato	avessero creduto	avessero dormito	fossero entrati(e)

For Irregular Verbs

essere	avere	tenere	capire
fossi stato(a)	avessi avuto	avessi tenuto	avessi capito
fossi stato(a)	avessi avuto	avessi tenuto	avessi capito
fosse stato(a)	avesse avuto	avesse tenuto	avesse capito
fossimo stati(e)	avessimo avuto	avessimo tenuto	avessimo capito
foste stati(e)	aveste avuto	aveste tenuto	aveste capito
fossero stati(e)	avessero avuto	avessero tenuto	avessero capito

N.B. Again how very easy! It is just like the past subjunctive, except here one uses the imperfect forms of **essere** and **avere** in the **congiuntivo**.

Section II. When to Use the Subjunctive

The subjunctive expresses the subjective, interior world of the speaker. It also expresses the probable as opposed to the definite. Below we will list eight categories in which the **congiuntivo** is called for. Read the examples only to be sure you understand them, not to memorize them. Try to get the flavor of situations in which the subjunctive is called for.

Sentences containing the subjunctive contain at least two clauses: an independent clause with a principal verb and a dependent clause with the subjunctive verb. The independent clause is usually in the indicative or conditional mood and can generally stand by itself, even if the dependent clause with the subjunctive were omitted, as in these examples:

Independent Clause Mood	Independent Clause	Dependent (Subjunctive) Clause
Indicative	I hope that ... Spero che ...	you will prepare lunch. tu PREPARI il pranzo.
	He thinks that ... Pensa che ...	she is intelligent. lei SIA intelligente.
Conditional	I would be rich ... Sarei ricco ...	if I were king. se io FOSSI re.

CALLS FOR THE SUBJUNCTIVE

Call 1: Verbs Expressing Emotional States

Principal verbs (verbs of the independent clause) expressing emotional states are usually followed by the subjunctive. Some of the most important of them are: **volere** - to wish; **desiderare** - to desire; **temere, avere paura** - to fear; **dubitare** - to doubt; **sperare** - to hope.

I hope that you will prepare lunch.
Spero che tu PREPARI il pranzo.

I want her to go (that she would go) there immediately.
Voglio che lei ci VADA subito.

Call 2: Verbs Expressing Thinking, Believing, Etc.

Principal verbs such as **pensare** - to think; **credere** - to believe; **parere, sembrare** - to seem, appear; **domandarsi, chiedersi** - to wonder, ask one's self; etc., take the subjunctive.

I <u>think</u> this is correct.
Penso che questo SIA giusto.

He <u>used to think</u> that it was impossible to reach the moon.
Credeva che FOSSE impossibile raggiungere la luna.

Call 3: The State of Not Knowing, Being Uncertain, Etc.

The state of not knowing, being uncertain (often expressed as a negative of a verb of knowing) is followed by the subjunctive. Such constructions include **non sapere** - to not know; **non essere sicuro** - to not be sure, etc. These same constructions in their positive form take the indicative.

I <u>am not sure</u> if (that) he is coming.
Non sono certo se (che) lui VENGA.

<u>But</u>

I <u>am sure</u> that he is coming.
Sono certo che lui <u>verrà</u>.

Call 4: Impersonal Verbs Indicating Probability, Etc.

There are many impersonal verbs indicating probability, necessity, urgency, propriety, etc., and they usually appear in the third-person singular, as in these examples: **è probabile che** - it is probable that; **bisogna che** or **è necessario che** - it is necessary that; **è urgente che** - it is urgent that.

Even though such statements are often issued as if they come from on high, remember that almost inevitably they express the subjective judgment of the speaker. Each of them could be preceded by "I think ...," e.g. "<u>I think</u> it <u>is probable that</u> (or <u>is necessary that</u>, <u>is urgent that</u>, etc.)" It is this implicit subjectivity that calls for the subjunctive in the dependent clause, as in these examples:

<u>It is necessary</u> that you write more.
Bisogna che tu SCRIVA di più.

<u>It was good</u> that Maria did the work.
Era bene che Maria FACESSE il lavoro.

<u>It is a pity</u> that she is not here.
Peccato che lei non SIA qui.

Here are some of the more common impersonal constructions
that take the subjunctive.

bisogna che	it is necessary that
occorre che	it is necessary that
peccato che	it is a pity that
è difficile che	it is difficult that
è giusto che	it is right (just) that
è importante che	it is important that
è meglio che	it is better that
è necessario che	it is necessary that
è probabile che	it is probable that
è urgente che	it is urgent that

Call 5: Conjunctions That Take the Subjunctive

Certain conjunctions are virtually always followed by the
subjunctive. As you can see, most of them are used in
constructions in which uncertainty and probabilty are implied,
hence the use of the subjunctive. Here are a few of them.

a condizione che	on the condition that
affinchè	so that, in order that
finchè	until
malgrado	despite the fact that
prima che	before + (verb clause)
purchè	so that, provided that
sebbene, benchè	although
senza che	without + (verb clause)

I will go with you <u>although</u> it may be cold.
Verrò con te **benchè** FACCIA freddo.

She will visit us <u>despite the fact</u> that Gianni isn't here.
Verrà a trovarci **malgrado che** Gianni non ci SIA.

I finished eating <u>before</u> they arrived.
Ho finito di mangiare **prima che** FOSSERO ARRIVATI.

Call 6: After Relative Superlatives and **Primo, Ultimo, Unico**

Recall that there are two forms of the superlative in
Italian: the relative superlative and the absolute superlative.
The <u>relative superlative</u> contrasts something with all others in
its category, e.g. "The <u>most beautiful</u> panorama (that) I have
seen." The <u>absolute superlative</u> makes no such comparisons, e.g.
"This is <u>a most beautiful</u> panorama."

In Italian, a clause following a relative superlative takes
the subjunctive, as in the following examples:

This is the <u>most beautiful</u> panorama that I have ever seen.
Questo è **il più bel** panorama che io ABBIA mai VISTO.

It was the <u>least interesting</u> book that I have ever read.
Era il libro **meno interessante** che io AVESSI mai LETTO.

In Italian, also, dependent clauses following such words as **primo, ultimo, unico** take the subjunctive, as in these examples:

He is <u>the first</u> fellow who went out.
Lui è **il primo** ragazzo che SIA ANDATO fuori.

She is the <u>only girl</u> who (has) finished the homework.
Lei è **l'unica ragazza** che ABBIA FINITO il compito.

Call 7: Impersonal Expressions without Antecedents

Certain impersonal expressions with pronouns such as **qualcuno** and **qualcosa** that indicate the speaker is looking for someone or something but has not found it take the subjunctive in the dependent clause, as in these examples:

I am looking <u>for something</u> that cleans well.
Cerco **qualcosa** che PULISCA bene.

I am looking <u>for someone</u> who knows Florence.
Cerco **qualcuno** che CONOSCA Firenze.

<u>But</u>

I have found <u>someone</u> who knows Florence.
Ho trovato **qualcuno** che <u>conosce</u> Firenze.
(The person's been found, hence no subjunctive.)

Call 8: Subjunctives in Contrary-to-Fact Sentences

"Contrary-to-fact" constructions are those in which there is an assertion that is clearly hypothetical and does not correspond to reality, e.g. "If I were king,..." The contrary-to-fact clause is always in the subjunctive. The conclusion that proceeds from it, "... I would be rich," is always in the conditional. The order of the clauses can vary, e.g.:

<u>If I were</u> king, I <u>would be</u> very rich.
Se io FOSSI re, **sarei** molto ricco.

I <u>would be</u> very rich, <u>if I were</u> king.
Sarei molto ricco, se io FOSSI re.

If I had had the money, I would have gone to Italy.
Se io AVESSI AVUTO il denaro, **sarei andato** in Italia.

I would be very happy if she were coming.
Sarei molto contento se lei VENISSE.

You may have noted that the concordance between which form of the conditional and which form of the subjunctive used in these examples differs from that in sentences using the indicative and subjunctive. Don't worry about that now. The flowcharts will make everything abundantly clear.

Quiz on Calls for the Subjunctive

This quiz is to test the development of your intuition about when a subjunctive is called for. At the end of each sentence, there is a blank. If you think a subjunctive is called for in the dependent clause, write "Yes" in the blank; if you think it is not called for, write "No." Check the next page for the correct answers.

1. The government declared today that costs are rising. _____

2. He feared that she had been killed. _____

3. It is better that you leave immediately. _____

4. I don't know if (that) he is on his way. _____

5. That was the best ball game that I have ever seen. _____

6. He said that he found the book. _____

7. You wonder if you made a mistake? _____

8. It is a far, far better thing that I do. _____

9. It is Mozart who wrote that lovely concerto. _____

10. It is a pity that Mozart died so young. _____

11. Have you found someone who does windows? _____

12. Do you know that classes start Wednesday? _____

13. I'll call Dr. Pym, although you don't look sick. _____

14. He has a cold that won't go away. _____

15. It would make it easier if taxes were lowered. _____

16. The children left no doubt that they wanted a dog. _____

17. I wonder if you could come see me tonight. _____

18. It is necessary that you keep working. _____

19. She is the most daring woman that I have seen. _____

20. He dealt the hand that won the game. _____

Answers to Quiz on Calls for the Subjunctive

The sentences of the quiz are shown below, with answers. For all "Yes" answers, the Call Number governing its choice is given so that you can check back.

```
 1. The government declared today that costs are rising.   (No)
 2. He feared that she had been killed.                    (Yes; 1)
 3. It is better that you leave immediately.               (Yes; 4)
 4. I don't know if (that) he is on his way.               (Yes; 3)
 5. That was the best ball game that I have ever seen.     (Yes; 6)

 6. He said that he found the book.                        (No)
 7. You wonder if you made a mistake?                      (Yes; 2)
 8. It is a far, far better thing that I do.               (Yes; 4)
 9. It is Mozart who wrote that lovely concerto.           (No)
10. It is a pity that Mozart died so young.                (Yes; 4)

11. Have you found someone who does windows?               (Yes; 7)
12. Do you know that classes start Wednesday?              (No)
13. I'll call Dr. Pym, although you don't look sick.       (Yes; 5)
14. He has a cold that won't go away.                      (No)
15. It would make it easier if taxes were lowered.         (Yes; 8)

16. The children left no doubt that they wanted a dog.     (No)
17. I wonder if you could come see me tonight.             (Yes; 2)
18. It is necessary that you keep working.                 (Yes; 4)
19. She's the most daring woman that I have seen.          (Yes; 6)
20. He dealt the hand that won the game.                   (No)
```

Section III. The Flowcharts

THREE KINDS OF COMPOUND SENTENCES

In Section II we described these three basic kinds of sentences that call for the subjunctive:

1. Those in which the main clause verb is a <u>conditional</u> (Call 8), usually found in "Contrary-to-Fact" or "Hypothetical" sentences, e.g.:

> I <u>would be</u> very rich, <u>if I were</u> king.
> **Sarei** molto ricco, se io FOSSI re.

The <u>would be</u> or **sarei** is the conditional part of the sentence.

2. Those in which the dependent clause is introduced by a <u>conjunction</u> that calls for a subjunctive (Call 5), e.g.:

> I will go with you <u>although</u> I don't feel well.
> Verrò con te **sebbene** non mi SENTA bene.

3. All the rest (Calls 1-4, 6-7), including sentences indicating feeling, thinking, doubting, impersonal probability and necessity, relative superlatives, and impersonal expressions without antecedents.

Shortly we will make the distinction between compound sentences in which the subjects of the two clauses are the <u>same</u>, e.g.:

> <u>I</u> will go with you although <u>I</u> don't feel well.

and those where the subjects are <u>different</u>, e.g.:

> <u>I</u> will go with you although <u>the weather</u> is bad.

For sentences involving a <u>conditional</u> or a <u>conjunction</u> <u>that calls for the subjunctive</u>, the first two just cited, it makes <u>no difference</u> whether the subjects are the same or different: A subjunctive is called for in either case.

For <u>all the others</u> (Calls 1-4, 6-7), which comprise about 80% of cases you will come up against, it <u>does</u> make a difference: If the subjects are the <u>same</u>, you will use an <u>infinitive</u>; if they are <u>different</u>, you will use something else, usually a subjunctive.

This means you will have to make a preselection as you begin to use the Pre-flowchart Flowchart. In the first column, "DETERMINING CLAUSE," you are asked to decide whether you are dealing with a <u>conditional</u> (Call 8) or a <u>conjunction</u> (Call 5) or something else. Once you have made this determination, you can then go on to analyze the rest of the sentence for the attributes determined by the four questions that follow.

FOUR NECESSARY QUESTIONS

For compound sentences that might require a subjunctive, four questions must be asked, namely:

1. Are the subjects of the clauses the same or different?

2. Is the mood of the verb in the main clause indicative or conditional?

3. Is the tense or form of the verb in the main clause present or past (for conditionals, simple or compound)?

4. Are the actions in the clauses simultaneous or not?

Each determination is an easy one to make, and each one sends you along one branch or another of a decision-making tree. At the tip of each branch is the fruit you are seeking: the proper verb form to use under the circumstances. Most of these verb forms will be in the subjunctive, of course, for that is the topic of this chapter; some will not be, and you of course must know them, too.

As with any rigid system, there will be exceptions, but the rules shown here will be right more than 80% of the time. Once you have mastered these rules, you will be in a better position to understand the exceptions.

The decision-making tree will be partially described in the text. It will be given in its more nearly complete form in the flowcharts that accompany the text.

DEFINITIONS AND DECISIONS

Subjects Same or Different?

Here are six sample sentences; subjects in the clauses are underlined.

1. <u>He</u> thinks that <u>he</u> is going to Rome.
2. <u>I</u> am happy that <u>I</u> know Lisa.
3. <u>We</u> hoped that <u>we</u> would be coming home.

4. He thinks that <u>Gianni</u> is going to Rome.
5. <u>I</u> am happy that <u>you</u> know Lisa.
6. <u>We</u> hoped that <u>Carlo</u> would be coming home.

In the first three sentences, the subjects of the clauses are <u>the same</u>, e.g. "He - he"; "I - I"; "We - we." In the last three, they are <u>different</u>, e.g. "He - Gianni"; "I - you"; "We - Carlo."

You will note, too, that the verbs in the main (independent) clauses (which we will always place at the beginning of the sentence in this chapter) are verbs often calling for the subjunctive in the dependent clause, e.g. "to think," "to be happy," "to hope."

When the subjects are <u>the same</u>, one uses an <u>infinitive</u>; when they are <u>different</u>, one uses something else. Look at the top of the Pre-flowchart Flowchart. You will note that, after the preselection for <u>conditionals</u> and <u>conjunctions</u> (Calls 8 and 5), for all other cases (Calls 1-4, 6-7), when subjects are <u>the same</u>, you are directed to Chart I, to find the right form of the infinitive. When they are <u>different</u>, you are directed to subsequent charts.

You are not yet quite ready to use Chart I, because the issue of simultaneity is raised on it -- an issue we will address shortly. Still, take a look at the Pre-flowchart Flowchart and Chart I, to begin to familiarize yourself with them.

Main Verb Mood

Main verbs are in one of three moods, namely, the <u>indicative</u>, the <u>imperative</u>, or the <u>conditional</u>. The imperative is handled the same as the indicative for our purposes, so our next decision is between just two possibilities: indicative (including imperative) vs. conditional. In the first three sentences to be given, the main verbs are in the indicative; in the next three they are in the conditional.

Indicative

He <u>thinks</u> Gianni is going to Rome.
I <u>am</u> happy that you knew Lisa.
<u>Be</u> happy that you know Lisa!
We <u>hoped</u> that Carlo was coming.

Conditional

He <u>would think</u> that Gianni is going to Rome.
I <u>would be</u> happy if you had known Lisa.
We <u>would hope</u> that Carlo had come.

THE PRE-FLOWCHART FLOWCHART

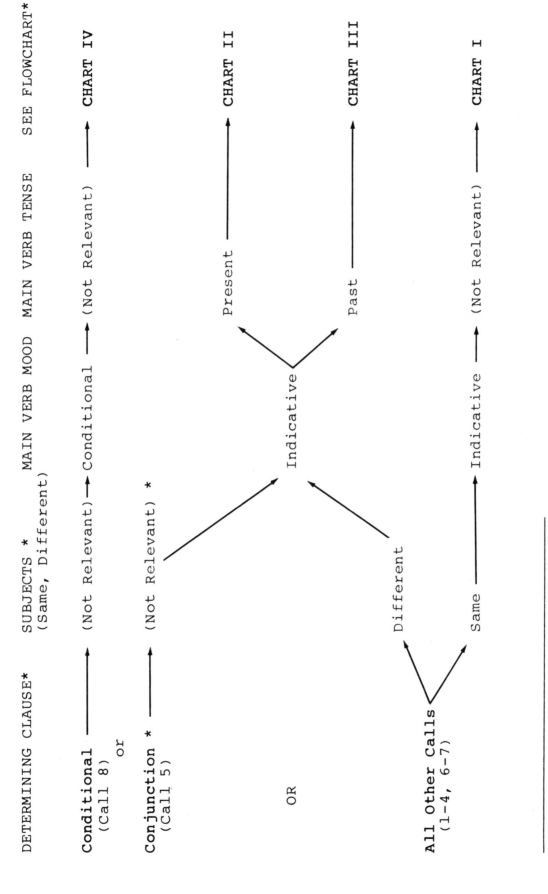

DETERMINING CLAUSE*   SUBJECTS *   MAIN VERB MOOD   MAIN VERB TENSE   SEE FLOWCHART*
                       (Same, Different)

Conditional   (Not Relevant) ⟶ Conditional ⟶ (Not Relevant) ⟶ **CHART IV**
(Call 8)
            or

Conjunction *   (Not Relevant) *
(Call 5)
                                          ⟶ Indicative

                                                     Present ⟶ **CHART II**

                                                     Past ⟶ **CHART III**

                      Different

              OR

All Other Calls   Same ⟶ Indicative ⟶ (Not Relevant) ⟶ **CHART I**
(1-4, 6-7)

---

   * Flowcharts I-III assume that the Subjunctive is NOT determined by a
Conditional (Call 8) or Conjunction (Call 5), and that the distinction between same or
different subjects is relevant. It if IS determined by a Conjunction or Conditional, the
distinction is NOT relevant and warnings about it at the tops of Charts I-III should be
ignored.

209

CHART I. SUBJECTS IN THE TWO CLAUSES ARE THE SAME

SUMMARY THUS FAR

1. Subjects in the two clauses are the same. (If they are different, you should be on Charts II or III.)

2. Main clause verb is in the indicative. (If it is in the conditional -- Call 8 -- you should be on Chart IV.)

3. Main clause not introduced by a conjunction. (If it is -- Call 5 -- you should be on Charts II or III, depending on the tense of the verb.)

EXAMPLES

1. He thinks (now) that he is going (now) to Rome.
2. I was happy (last year) that I knew Lisa (last year).
3. He thinks (now) that he has been in Rome (in the past).
4. I was happy (last year) that I had known Lisa (two years ago).

SIMULTANEITY

Actions in the two clauses can be simultaneous (as in Example 1, 2) or non-simultaneous (as in Example 3, 4). If the actions are simultaneous, use the Present Infinitive; if they are non-simultaneous, use the Past Infinitive.

Simultaneity

Simultaneous

Non-Simultaneous

VERB FORM TO USE

PRESENT INFINITIVE

1. Lui pensa (ora) **di andare** (ora) a Roma.

2. Ero felice (l'anno scorso) **di conoscere** Lisa (l'anno scorso).

PAST INFINITIVE

3. Lui pensa (ora) **di essere stato** a Roma (nel passato).

4. Ero felice (l'anno scorso) **di aver conosciuto** Lisa (due anni fa).

210

As you can see from the Pre-flowchart Flowchart, when the main verb is in the indicative, one is referred to Charts II and III for further determinations. When it is in the conditional, one is referred to Chart IV.

Tenses and Forms

<u>Tenses for the Indicative</u>. There are three kinds of tenses in the indicative: present, future, and past (in one of its several forms). For our purposes, the future is a part of the present, so the basic determination to be made for the main clause verb is: <u>present (including future)</u> vs. <u>past</u>. See these examples:

<u>Present</u>

He <u>thinks</u> Gianni is going to Rome.
I <u>am</u> happy that you knew Lisa.
We (<u>will</u>) <u>hope</u> that Carlo has come.

<u>Past</u>

He <u>thought</u> that Gianni was going to Rome.
I <u>was</u> happy that you knew Lisa.
We <u>had hoped</u> that Carlo had already come.

As you will note from the Pre-flowchart Flowchart, indicatives in the <u>present</u> are handled on Chart II, and those in the <u>past</u> are handled on Chart III.

<u>Forms for Conditionals</u>. Rather than having tenses, the conditional has two <u>forms</u>, namely the <u>simple</u> and the <u>compound</u>, as shown in these examples.

<u>Simple</u>

He <u>would think</u> that Gianni is going to Rome.
I <u>would be</u> happy if you knew Lisa.
We <u>would hope</u> that Carlo has come.

<u>Compound</u>

He <u>would have thought</u> that Gianni had gone to Rome.
I <u>would have been</u> happy if you had known Lisa.
We <u>would have hoped</u> that Carlo had come.

Conditionals of any form are dealt with on Chart IV.

Simultaneity

The fourth and last determination to be made is of simultaneity of actions in the two clauses: Are they occurring at the same time or not? See these examples:

<u>Simultaneous</u>

He thinks (<u>now</u>) that Gianni is going (<u>now</u>) to Rome.
I was happy (<u>then</u>) that you knew Lisa (<u>then</u>).
We were hoping (<u>then</u>) that Carlo was coming (<u>then</u>).

<u>Non-Simultaneous</u>

He thinks (<u>now</u>) that Gianni will go (<u>tomorrow</u>) to Rome.
I was happy (<u>yesterday</u>) that you had known Lisa (<u>last year</u>).
We hoped (<u>in April</u>) that Carlo would come (<u>in May</u>).

Take a look at the non-simultaneous examples. In the first, the action in the dependent clause (tomorrow) takes place <u>after</u> that of the independent or main clause (now). In the second it took place <u>before</u> (last year) that of the main clause (yesterday). In the third, the dependent-clause action takes place <u>after</u> (in May) that of the main clause (in April).

Prof. Orvieto told us that "the conditional is the past's window on the future." That is, in Italian as in English, if the action in the dependent clause took place <u>after</u> the action in the main clause but before now, one anticipates it by using the conditional, e.g.:

We hoped in April that Carlo <u>would come</u> in May.
Abbiamo sperato in Aprile che Carlo **sarebbe venuto** in Maggio.

But that window looks only up to the present moment. If the contemplated action has not occurred before now, in Italian one uses the indicative, e.g.:

We hoped in April that Carlo <u>would come</u> (<u>comes</u>) tomorrow.
Abbiamo sperato in Aprile che Carlo **verrà** (**viene**) domani.

If, however, the actions were <u>simultaneous</u>, <u>or</u> if the action in the dependent clause took place <u>before</u> that of the main clause, then one uses a subjunctive, e.g.:

We hoped in April that Carlo was coming in April.
Abbiamo sperato in Aprile che Carlo ARRIVASSE in Aprile.

<u>Or</u>

We hoped in April that Carlo had (already) come in March.
Abbiamo sperato in Aprile che Carlo
FOSSE già ARRIVATO in Marzo.

So we have two orders of decisions to make in considering simultaneity: (1) Are the actions simultaneous or not? (2) If not, does the action in the dependent clause come before or after that of the main clause?

If the actions are simultaneous, we use the subjunctive.

If the actions are not simultaneous, if that in the dependent clause comes before that in the main clause, we still use the subjunctive; but if the action of the dependent clause comes after that of the main clause, we use either a conditional or an indicative.

Just which forms of the subjunctive, conditional, or indicative one uses are given in Charts II and III.

Visualizing all this from just words is very difficult, so take a look now at Charts II, III, and IV.

SUMMARY OF THE FLOWCHARTS

Starting with the Pre-flowchart Flowchart, go through the flowcharts again, to see if it all makes sense, to see if the progression from each choice point to the next is clear. Then look at Chart V, which summarizes the preceding charts. Soon you will be taking quizzes on the subjunctive, and we will ask you to cite which of Charts I through IV you used in making each of your decisions. If you use Chart V for the quizzes and do it successfully, obviously you have mastered the preceding charts.

CHART II. MAIN VERB IS IN <u>INDICATIVE, PRESENT OR FUTURE TENSE</u>

SUMMARY THUS FAR

1. <u>Subjects</u> of the clauses are <u>different</u>.* (If they are the same, you should be on Chart I.)

2. The main verb <u>mood</u> is <u>indicative</u> (or <u>imperative</u>). (If it is conditional, you should be on Chart IV.)

3. The main verb tense is <u>present</u> (or <u>future</u>). (If it is past, you should be on Chart III.)

EXAMPLES

1. He thinks (now) that Gianni is going (now) to Rome.
2. I am happy (now) that you knew Lisa (then).
3. We hope (now) that Carlo will come (tomorrow).

SIMULTANEITY

Actions in the two clauses can be <u>simultaneous</u> (Example 1) or <u>non-simultaneous</u>. If they are simultaneous, use the Present Subjunctive. If non-simultaneous, that of the dependent clause can precede or follow that of main clause. If it <u>precedes</u> (Example 2), use the Past <u>Subjunctive</u>; if it <u>follows</u> (Example 3), use the <u>Indicative</u>.

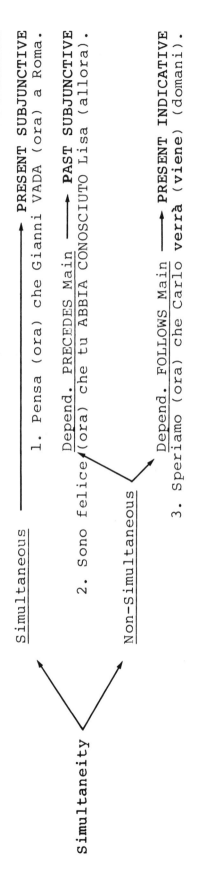

VERB FORM TO USE

<u>Simultaneous</u> ——————————→ **PRESENT SUBJUNCTIVE**

1. Pensa (ora) che Gianni VADA (ora) a Roma.

<u>Depend. PRECEDES Main</u> ——→ **PAST SUBJUNCTIVE**

2. Sono felice (ora) che tu ABBIA CONOSCIUTO Lisa (allora).

<u>Non-Simultaneous</u>

<u>Depend. FOLLOWS Main</u> ——→ **PRESENT INDICATIVE**

3. Speriamo (ora) che Carlo **verrà** (**viene**) (domani).

Simultaneity

---

* See footnote on the Pre-flowchart Flowchart.

CHART III. MAIN VERB IS IN INDICATIVE, ANY PAST TENSE

SUMMARY THUS FAR

1. Subjects of the clauses are different.* (If they are the same, you should be on Chart I.)

2. The main verb mood is indicative (or imperative). (If it is conditional, you should be on Chart IV.)

3. The main verb tense is past (in any of its forms). (If it is present or future, you should be on Chart II.)

EXAMPLES

1. He thought (then) that Gianni was going (then) to Rome.
2. I was happy (last week) that you had known Lisa (last year).
3. We had hoped (last year) that Carlo would come (this year).

SIMULTANEITY

Actions in the two clauses can be simultaneous (Example 1) or non-simultaneous. If they are simultaneous, use the Imperfect Subjunctive. If non-simultaneous, (Examples 2, 3) that of dependent clause can precede or follow that of main clause. If it precedes (Example 2), use the Pluperfect Subjunctive; if it follows (Example 3), use the compound conditional.

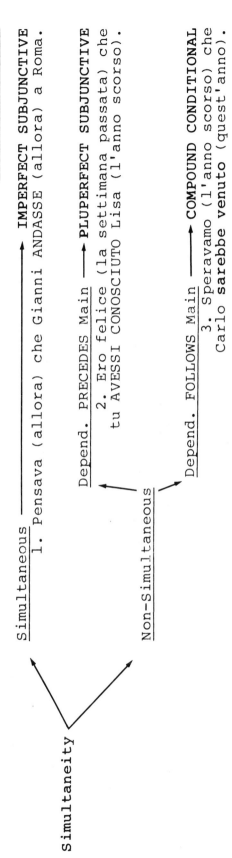

VERB FORM TO USE

Simultaneous
1. Pensava (allora) che Gianni ANDASSE (allora) a Roma. → **IMPERFECT SUBJUNCTIVE**

Non-Simultaneous

Depend. PRECEDES Main → **PLUPERFECT SUBJUNCTIVE**
2. Ero felice (la settimana passata) che tu AVESSI CONOSCIUTO Lisa (l'anno scorso).

Depend. FOLLOWS Main → **COMPOUND CONDITIONAL**
3. Speravamo (l'anno scorso) che Carlo **sarebbe venuto** (quest'anno).

Simultaneity

* See footnote on Pre-flowchart Flowchart.

215

CHART IV.   MAIN VERB IS IN CONDITIONAL

SUMMARY THUS FAR

1. Subjects of the clauses may be the same or different.

2. The main verb mood is conditional. (If the main verb mood is indicative or imperative, you should be on Charts I-III.)

EXAMPLES

1. I would be happy (now) if you knew Lisa (now).
2. I would be happy (now) if you had known Lisa (last year).
3. I would have been happy (last year) if you had known Lisa (two years ago).
4. We would have hoped (yesterday) that Carlo had already come.

FORM AND SIMULTANEITY

Things are a little different here than with main verbs in the indicative. The only combination that will lead to an imperfect subjunctive is a simple conditional in the main clause and an imperfect subjunctive in the dependent clause, as in Example 1. Any compound conditional in the main clause and/or any compound past in the dependent clause leads to a pluperfect subjunctive.

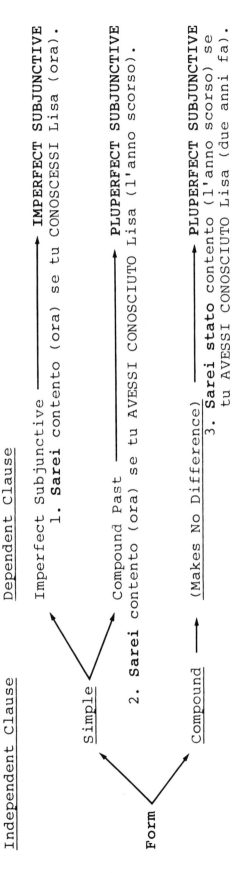

VERB FORM TO USE

Independent Clause

Simple

Compound

Form

Dependent Clause

Imperfect Subjunctive → IMPERFECT SUBJUNCTIVE
1. **Sarei** contento (ora) se tu CONOSCESSI Lisa (ora).

Compound Past → PLUPERFECT SUBJUNCTIVE
2. **Sarei** contento (ora) se tu AVESSI CONOSCIUTO Lisa (l'anno scorso).

(Makes No Difference) → PLUPERFECT SUBJUNCTIVE
3. **Sarei stato** contento (l'anno scorso) se tu AVESSI CONOSCIUTO Lisa (due anni fa).

4. Avremmo sperato (ieri) che Carlo FOSSE già VENUTO (ARRIVATO).

216

CHART V. SUMMARY OF CHARTS I-IV

A. SUBJECTS OF CLAUSES: SAME OR DIFFERENT?
   (If same, stay here with A; if different, go below to B.)

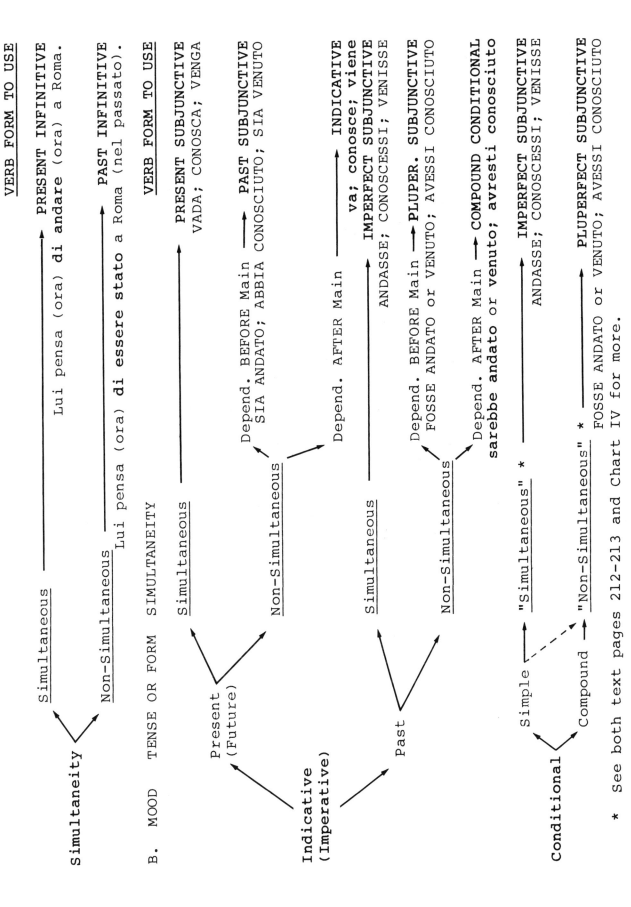

B. MOOD   TENSE OR FORM   SIMULTANEITY

* See both text pages 212-213 and Chart IV for more.

Miniquiz on Determining Subjunctives

We're going to give you a miniquiz here, to warm you up for a rather tougher one shortly. In the miniquiz, each item will be in three parts:

(1) A sentence in English to be translated.

(2) Spaces for you to write your determinations of the several factors that need to be decided upon. Just before the quiz, we will suggest abbreviations for you to use for each of these factors. The factors and spaces will appear as follows:

Sub __   Mood __   Ten/Form ___   Flc ___   Sim ____   Verb _____

The factors are these:

      (a) Sub = Subjects of the clauses: same or different?
      (b) Mood = Mood of the <u>main</u> clause verb
      (c) Ten/Form = Tense or Form of the <u>main</u> clause verb
      (d) Flc = Flowchart number for proper determination
      (e) Sim = Simultaneity of actions
      (f) Verb = Mood and form of proper verb for the <u>dependent</u> clause

(3) A space for the Italian translation. When you have completed the quiz, check against the answers on the following pages.

Abbreviations for the Quiz. Use the abbreviations shown
here to fill in the blanks. The same abbreviations will be used
for the answers.

    Subjects:

        S = same
        D = different

Mood of Main Clause Verb:

        I = indicative or imperative
        C = conditional

Tenses and Forms of Main Clause Verb:

        Pr = present tense
        Ft = future tense
        Pa = past tense (any)

        Si = simple conditional
        Cp = compound conditional

Flowchart Number: Use a Roman numeral from I through IV

Simultaneity:

        Slt = simultaneous
        Non = non-simultaneous

Verb for Dependant Clause:

        Pr Sub = present subjunctive
        Im Sub = imperfect subjunctive
        Pa Sub = past subjunctive
        Pl Sub = pluperfect subjunctive

        Pr Inf = present infinitive
        Pa Inf = past infinitive

    Fill in the blanks and translate the first question. Then
check your work against the answers and explanation that follows.

1. I was happy that Maria was indoors.

Sub __   Mood __   Ten/Form ___   Flc ___   Sim ____   Verb _____

Italian _____

1. I was happy that Maria was indoors.

Sub <u>D</u>   Mood <u>I</u>   Ten/Form <u>Pa</u>   Flc <u>III</u>   Sim <u>Slt</u>   Verb <u>Im Sub</u>

Italian   <u>Ero contento che Maria FOSSE dentro.</u>

     The reasons for the entries in the blanks is as follows: The subjects were different ("I" - "Maria"), so a "D" was entered in the first blank. The mood of the main verb was indicative, so for "Mood," an "I" was entered. The tense was past, hence "Pa" was entered. This combination directs you to Chart III. The actions were simultaneous, hence "Slt." The Chart therefore directs you to choose an imperfect subjunctive, hence "Im Sub."

     The imperfect subjunctive of **essere** in this case is FOSSE, hence the construction of the Italian sentence.

     And now for the remainder of the miniquiz.

2. It is better that he doesn't go.

Sub __   Mood __   Ten/Form ___   Flc ___   Sim ____   Verb _____

Italian _____

3. I would answer the phone if it were to ring.

Sub __   Mood __   Ten/Form ___   Flc ___   Sim ____   Verb _____

Italian _____

4. He is sad that he has lost his girlfriend.

Sub __   Mood __   Ten/Form ___   Flc ___   Sim ____   Verb _____

Italian _____

5. It would be better if he had finished the test.

Sub __   Mood __   Ten/Form ___   Flc ___   Sim ____   Verb _____

Italian _____

6. Are you happy that she did not arrive?

Sub __   Mood __   Ten/Form ___   Flc ___   Sim ____   Verb _____

Italian _____

7. Although I am broke (**essere al verde**), I will go with you.

Sub __   Mood __   Ten/Form ___   Flc ___   Sim ____   Verb _____

Italian _____

8. Before they came, she (had) prepared dinner.

Sub __   Mood __   Ten/Form ___   Flc ___   Sim ____   Verb _____

Italian _____

9. She is the most pleasant person I have ever met.

Sub __   Mood __   Ten/Form ___   Flc ___   Sim ____   Verb _____

Italian _____

10. Maria thinks that Gianni is hungry.

Sub __   Mood __   Ten/Form ___   Flc ___   Sim ____   Verb _____

Italian _____

Answers to Miniquiz on Determining Subjunctives

1. I was happy that Maria was indoors.

Sub <u>D</u>   Mood <u>I</u>   Ten/Form <u>Pa</u>   Flc <u>III</u>   Sim <u>Slt</u>   Verb <u>Im Sub</u>

    Ero contento che Maria FOSSE dentro.

2. It is better that he doesn't go.

Sub <u>D</u>   Mood <u>I</u>   Ten/Form <u>Pr</u>   Flc <u>II</u>   Sim <u>Slt</u>   Verb <u>Pr Sub</u>

    E' meglio che lui non VADA.

3. I would answer the phone if it were to ring.

Sub <u>D</u>   Mood <u>C</u>   Ten/Form <u>Si</u>   Flc <u>IV</u>   Sim <u>Slt</u>   Verb <u>Im Sub</u>

    Risponderei al telefono se SUONASSE.

4. He is sad that he has lost his girlfriend.

Sub <u>S</u>   Mood <u>I</u>   Ten/Form <u>Pr</u>   Flc <u>I</u>   Sim <u>Non</u>   Verb <u>Pa Inf</u>

   Lui è triste **di aver perso (perduto)** la sua ragazza.

5. It would be better if he had finished the test.

Sub <u>D</u>   Mood <u>C</u>   Ten/Form <u>Si</u>   Flc <u>IV</u>   Sim <u>Non</u>   Verb <u>Pl Sub</u>

   Sarebbe (stato) meglio che lui AVESSE FINITO l'esame.

6. Are you happy that she did not arrive?

Sub <u>D</u>   Mood <u>I</u>   Ten/Form <u>Pr</u>   Flc <u>II</u>   Sim <u>Non</u>   Verb <u>Pa Sub</u>

   Sei felice che lei non SIA ARRIVATA?

7. Although I am broke, I will go with you. *

Sub <u>S</u>   Mood <u>I</u>   Ten/Form <u>Pr</u>   Flc <u>II</u>   Sim <u>Slt</u>   Verb <u>Pr Sub</u>

   Sebbene io SIA al verde, verrò con te.

8. Before they came, she (had) prepared dinner.

Sub <u>D</u>   Mood <u>I</u>   Ten/Form <u>Pa</u>   Flc <u>III</u>   Sim <u>Non</u>   Verb <u>Pl Sub</u>

   Prima che FOSSERO ARRIVATI, lei aveva preparato la cena.

9. She is the most pleasant person I have ever met.

Sub <u>D</u>   Mood <u>I</u>   Ten/Form <u>Pr</u>   Flc <u>II</u>   Sim <u>Non</u>   Verb <u>Pa Sub</u>

   Lei è la persona più piacevole che io ABBIA mai INCONTRATO.

10. Maria thinks that Gianni is hungry.

Sub <u>D</u>   Mood <u>I</u>   Ten/Form <u>Pr</u>   Flc <u>II</u>   Sim <u>Slt</u>   Verb <u>Pr Sub</u>

   Maria pensa che Gianni ABBIA fame.

---

   * This is an example of where a <u>conjunction</u> ("although")
determines the necessity for the subjunctive, in spite of the fact
that the subjects are the same in both clauses; see Call 5.

A Tougher Quiz on Determining Subjunctives

Now you will be given 14 more sentences to analyze and translate, as you just were doing. Some of them will be a bit more complex, however. When you have completed them, check the answers on the following pages.

We will repeat the abbreviations to use for the blanks.

Subjects:

    S = same
    D = different

Mood of Main Clause Verb:

    I = indicative or imperative
    C = conditional

Tenses and Forms of Main Clause Verb:

    Pr = present tense
    Ft = future tense
    Pa = past tense (any)

    Si = simple conditional
    Cp = compound conditional

Flowchart Number: Use a Roman numeral from I through IV

Simultaneity:

    Slt = simultaneous
    Non = non-simultaneous

Verb for Dependant Clause:

    Pr Sub = present subjunctive
    Im Sub = imperfect subjunctive
    Pa Sub = past subjunctive
    Pl Sub = pluperfect subjunctive

    Pr Inf = present infinitive
    Pa Inf = past infinitive

1. She would have studied these verbs if she had known the rules.*

Sub ___   Mood ___   Ten/Form ___   Flc ___   Sim ___   Verb _____

Italian _____

2. It is possible that you may be tired.

Sub ___   Mood ___   Ten/Form ___   Flc ___   Sim ___   Verb _____

Italian _____

3. Mary was wondering whether Elena had gone out with Luigi.

Sub ___   Mood ___   Ten/Form ___   Flc ___   Sim ___   Verb _____

Italian _____

4. Although it was cold, they went to the beach.

Sub ___   Mood ___   Ten/Form ___   Flc ___   Sim ___   Verb _____

Italian _____

5. They were afraid that John had lost his way.

Sub ___   Mood ___   Ten/Form ___   Flc ___   Sim ___   Verb _____

Italian _____

6. I do not think that he has left.

Sub ___   Mood ___   Ten/Form ___   Flc ___   Sim ___   Verb _____

Italian _____

7. He will be sorry that you have not waited for him.

Sub ___   Mood ___   Ten/Form ___   Flc ___   Sim ___   Verb _____

Italian _____

_____

   * Note that when the main verb is in the <u>conditional</u>, even though both subjects are the same, the <u>subjunctive</u> will be called for in the dependent clause.

8. She is happy that they may be going to Italy this summer.

Sub __   Mood __   Ten/Form ___   Flc ___   Sim ____   Verb _____

Italian _____

9. They would have gone with Mary if there had been more seats.

Sub __   Mood __   Ten/Form ___   Flc ___   Sim ____   Verb _____

Italian _____

10. He wanted me to (that I would) sing.

Sub __   Mood __   Ten/Form ___   Flc ___   Sim ____   Verb _____

Italian _____

11. It is important that you (**voi**) read this article.

Sub __   Mood __   Ten/Form ___   Flc ___   Sim ____   Verb _____

Italian _____

12. I will not go to the beach unless the weather is really hot. *

Sub __   Mood __   Ten/Form ___   Flc ___   Sim ____   Verb _____

Italian _____ *

13. If you (**tu**) had read more books, you'd know more about Italy. **

Sub __   Mood __   Ten/Form ___   Flc ___   Sim ____   Verb _____

Italian _____ **

14. I didn't believe that Elena had read the book.

Sub __   Mood __   Ten/Form ___   Flc ___   Sim ____   Verb _____

Italian _____

_____

   * Unless is translated **a meno che** + (subject) + **non** +
(predicate). In this case, ... **a meno che** il tempo **non** + (fare)
proprio caldo.

   ** Note that when the main verb is in the conditional, even
though both subjects are the same, the subjunctive will be called
for in the dependent clause.

Answers to Tougher Quiz on Determining Subjunctives

1. She would have studied these verbs if she had known the rules.

Sub <u>S</u>   Mood <u>C</u>   Ten/Form <u>Cp</u>   Flc <u>IV</u>   Sim <u>Non</u>   Verb <u>Pl Sub</u>

   Avrebbe studiato questi verbi se lei AVESSE SAPUTO queste regole.

2. It is possible that you may be tired.

Sub <u>D</u>   Mood <u>I</u>   Ten/Form <u>Pr</u>   Flc <u>II</u>   Sim <u>Slt</u>   Verb <u>Pr Sub</u>

   E' possibile che tu SIA stanco.

3. Mary was wondering whether Elena had gone out with Luigi.

Sub <u>D</u>   Mood <u>I</u>   Ten/Form <u>Pa</u>   Flc <u>III</u>   Sim <u>Non</u>   Verb <u>Pl Sub</u>

   Maria si domandava se Elena FOSSE USCITA con Luigi.

4. Although it was cold, they went to the beach.

Sub <u>D</u>   Mood <u>I</u>   Ten/Form <u>Pa</u>   Flc <u>III</u>   Sim <u>Slt</u>   Verb <u>Im Sub</u>

   Sabbene FACESSE freddo, sono andati alla spiaggia.

5. They were afraid that John had lost his way.

Sub <u>D</u>   Mood <u>I</u>   Ten/Form <u>Pa</u>   Flc <u>III</u>   Sim <u>Non</u>   Verb <u>Pl Sub</u>

   Avevano paura (temevano) che John AVESSE PERSO la via.

6. I do not think that he has left.

Sub <u>D</u>   Mood <u>I</u>   Ten/Form <u>Pr</u>   Flc <u>II</u>   Sim <u>Non</u>   Verb <u>Pa Sub</u>

   Non credo che lui SIA PARTITO.

7. He will be sorry that you have not waited for him.

Sub <u>D</u>   Mood <u>I</u>   Ten/Form <u>Ft</u>   Flc <u>II</u>   Sim <u>Non</u>   Verb <u>Pa Sub</u>

   Gli dispiacerà che tu non lo ABBIA ASPETTATO.

8. She is happy that they may be going to Italy this summer.

Sub <u>D</u>   Mood <u>I</u>   Ten/Form <u>Pr</u>   Flc <u>II</u>   Sim <u>Slt</u>   Verb <u>Pr Sub</u>

   Lei è felice che VADANO in Italia quest'estate.

9. They would have gone if there had been more seats.

Sub <u>D</u>   Mood <u>C</u>   Ten/Form <u>Cp</u>   Flc <u>IV</u>   Sim <u>Slt</u>   Verb <u>Pl Sub</u>

   Sarebbero andati se ci FOSSERO STATI più posti.

10. He wanted me to (that I would) sing.

Sub <u>D</u>   Mood <u>I</u>   Ten/Form <u>Pa</u>   Flc <u>III</u>   Sim <u>Slt</u>   Verb <u>Im Sub</u>

   Voleva che io CANTASSI.

11. It is important that you (**voi**) read this article.

Sub <u>D</u>   Mood <u>I</u>   Ten/Form <u>Pr</u>   Flc <u>II</u>   Sim <u>Slt</u>   Verb <u>Pr Sub</u>

   E' importante che voi LEGGIATE quest'articolo.

12. I will not go to the beach unless the weather is really hot.

Sub <u>D</u>   Mood <u>I</u>   Ten/Form <u>Ft</u>   Flc <u>II</u>   Sim <u>Slt</u>   Verb <u>Pr Sub</u>

Non andrò alla spiaggia a meno che il tempo non FACCIA
proprio caldo.

13. If you (**tu**) had read more books, you'd know more about Italy.

Sub <u>S</u>   Mood <u>C</u>   Ten/Form <u>Pa</u>   Flc <u>IV</u>   Sim <u>Non</u>   Verb <u>Pl Sub</u>

   Se tu AVESSI LETTO più libri, avresti saputo di più
sull'Italia.

14. I didn't believe that Elena had read the book.

Sub <u>D</u>   Mood <u>I</u>   Ten/Form <u>Pa</u>   Flc <u>III</u>   Sim <u>Non</u>   Verb <u>Pl Sub</u>

   Non credevo che Elena AVESSE LETTO il libro.

   How did you do on this tougher quiz? If you got most of them
right, you are well on your way to mastering that most difficult
part of Italian, the subjunctive.

TWENTY.

AN
AFTERWORD

Now we have come to the end of the regular text of this book. If you discover new rules and patterns of your own, let me know about them. If we go on to a second edition, we may incorporate some of them and, if we do, your contribution will certainly be acknowledged.

Here's the final item for the book. The seventeenth-century Venetians adapted the word **schiavo** -- slave -- as a salutation with roughly the same meaning as "your obedient servant." That once obsequious and local usage is today the much more egalitarian and nearly universal ...

CIAO!

APPENDIX: ENGLISH WORDS CURRENT IN ITALY

Certain English words enjoy a certain vogue in Italy. Many of them are listed below. They are almost inevitably masculine and therefore preceded by **il** or **lo** in the singular. Pronunciations remain Italian: "hobby" is pronounced **"awe-bee"**; "killer" is **"keel-air."** As you can see, many of the words come from entertainment, sports, or travel.

alt (halt)	dance, -ing	in, out	record (music)
autobus	detective	(socially)	ring (boxing)
	drink		rock, -and roll
baby		jazz	(music)
babysitter	film	jukebox	
bar	flirt		self service
barbeque	folk (music)	killer	set (tennis)
basket(ball)	football		sexy
big	footing	leader (world)	shopping
boom (economic)	(jogging)		slogan
box (garage)		manager	smog
Boy Scout	gangster	match (sports)	snob
brandy	garage		sport
bus	gin	off limits	staff
	goal	OK	star (movie)
chewing-gum	golf (sweater)		stop (sign)
clan (Mafia)	gorilla (body-	party (social)	sweater
club	guard)	performance	
Coca-Cola	gum	picnic	teen-ager
cocktail		pop (music)	
computer	hamburger	pullman (small	VIP
cowboy	handicapped	bus)	
crack (stock-	hobby	pullover	weekend
market fall)	hostel (youth)	(sweater)	western (movie)

Nouns, verbs, and Unfaithful Cognates are identified as such in this listing. The abbreviations used are as follows:

(f.) = feminine noun

(m.) = masculine noun

(m&f.) = masculine and/or feminine noun

* = Unfaithful Cognate

(v.) = plain verb, neither member of a family nor an -isco verb

(vf.) = verb which is a member of a family

(vsc.) = verb of -isco type

Verbs which are family members, that is, carry the "(vf.)" designation, are listed both individually in alphabetic order and again grouped as part of the families. For an example, see "**accedere** (vf.)," shown as the fifth entry and shown again under **cedere** as part of that family of verbs.

a to, at, in
abbracciare (v.), to embrace
abbraccio (m.), embrace
accadere (v.), to happen, occur
accedere (vf.), to approach, comply with
accendere (v.), to light, kindle
accidente (m.), accident, mishap
accidenti dammit
accludere (v.), to enclose, include
accogliere (vf.), to greet, welcome
accomodarsi (v.), to make one's self comfortable
accorgersi (v.), to notice
accorrere (vf.), to run, rush
accrescere (vf.), to increase
addurre (vf.), to adduce
adesso now
affisso (m.), affix
affrontare (v.)*, to face, confront
affronto (m.), affront
aggettivo (m.), adjective
aggiungere (vf.), to add
aiutare (v.), to help, aid
aiuto (m.), help, aid
allora then

altezza (f.), height
alzarsi (v.), to get up, rise up
alzata (f.), getting up, rising up
amare (v.), to love
ammettere (vf.), to admit
amore (m.), love
ancora still, yet
andare (v.), to go
anno (m.), year
annoiar(si) (v.)*, to be bored
antecedere (vf.), to precede
apertura (f.), aperture, opening
appartenere (vf.)*, to belong (to)
appendere (vf.), to append, hang up
apprendere (vf.)*, to learn
aprire (v.), to open
ardere (v.), to burn
argomento (m.)*, topic of discourse
arrivare (v.), to arrive
arrivo (m.), arrival
artista (m&f.), artist
ascendere (vf.), to ascend, climb
ascrivere (vf.), to ascribe
aspergere (v.)*, to sprinkle

aspettare (v.), to wait
assuefar(si) (vf.), to accustom,
    get used to
astrarre (vf.), to abstract
attendere (vf.)*, to await,
    expect
attener(si) (vf.)*, to stick
    with
attesa (f.), waiting
attimo (m.), moment
atto (m.), act
attrarre (vf.), to attract,
    draw
attuale* currently, now
avanti ahead, forward
avere (v.), to have
avvenire (vf.), to happen,
    occur
avviso (m.)*, notice, warning
avvocato (m.), lawyer, advocate
avvolgere (vf.), to wrap around
bambino(a) (m&f.), baby, child
battere (v.), to beat
bene well, good
benedire (vf.), to bless
benedizione (f.), benediction
benevolenza (f.), benevolence
bere (v.), to drink
bevuta (f.), drink, beverage
bibita (f.), drink, beverage
biblioteca (f.), library
bistecca (f.), steak, beefsteak
bravo* clever, good
breve brief, short
cambiare (v.), to change,
    exchange money
cambio (m.), change, money
    exchange
camera (f.)*, room
camminare (v.), to walk
capire (vsc.), to understand
capitare (v.), to happen
capovolgere (vf.), to turn
    upside down
caricare (v.), to charge, load
cedere (vf.), to cede, yield
  accedere to approach,
      comply with
  antecedere to precede
  concedere to concede
  decedere to die
  incedere to walk

precedere to precede
procedere to proceed
retrocedere to degrade
succedere* to happen
cento (m.), one hundred
cercare (v.), to seek, search
    for
chiacchierare (v.), to chat,
    gossip
chiamare (v.), to call
chiamata (f.), call, phone call
chiaro clear
chiudere (v.), to close
ci there, ourselves
cingere (v.), to cinch, gird
cinquanta (m.), fifty
cinque (m.), five
cioè that is
città (f.), city
clima (m.), climate
cogliere (vf.), to collect
coincidere (v.), to coincide
coinvolgere (vf.), to involve
    together
collina (f.), hill
cominciare (v.), to commence,
    begin
commesso(a) (m&f.), clerk
commettere (vf.), to commit
commuovere (vf.)*, to move
    emotionally
comporre (vf.), to compose
comprare (v.), to buy
comprendere (vf.), to
    comprise, include
comprimere (vf.), to compress
compromesso (m.), compromise
compromettere (vf.), to
    compromise
comunista (m&f.), communist
comunque however
concedere (vf.), to concede
concludere (v.), to conclude
conclusione (f.), conclusion
concorrere (vf.), to compete,
    concur
condurre (vf.), to conduct
  addurre to adduce
  dedurre to deduce, deduct
  indurre to induce
  introdurre to introduce
  produrre to produce

ridurre to reduce
sedurre to seduce
tradurre* to translate
conflitto (m.), conflict
confondere (v.), to confound,
    confuse
congiungere (vf.), to conjoin
conoscere (v.), to know a
    person or place
constatare (vf.), to ascertain
contendere (vf.), to contend
contenere (vf.), to contain
contentezza (f.), contentedness
continuare (v.), to continue
contraddire (vf.), to
    contradict
contraffare (vf.), to
    counterfeit
contrarre (vf.), to contract
contrastare (vf.), to contrast
contravvenire (vf.), to
    contravene
controllare (v.)*, to inspect,
    control
controllo (m.)*, inspection
convenire (vf.), to convene
coraggioso brave, courageous
correggere (v.), to correct
correre (vf.), to run
  accorrere to run, rush
  concorrere to compete,
      concur
  discorrere to discourse,
      chat
  occorrere* to be necessary
  ricorrere to recur, have
      recourse to
  soccorrere to succor, help
  trascorrere to pass time
cospicuo conspicuous
cospirare (v.), to conspire
costante constant
costare (vf.), to cost
costringere (v.), to constrain
costruire (vsc.), to
    construct, build
credere (v.), to believe
crescere (vf.), to increase,
    grow
  accrescere to increase
  decrescere to decrease
  rincrescere to regret

crescita (f.), growth
crisi (f.), crisis
cucina (f.), kitchen
cucinare (v.), to cook
cugino(a) (m&f.), cousin
da as, from
dare (v.), to give, confer
davanti (a) in front of
debole weak
decedere (vf.), to die
decrescere (vf.), to decrease
dedurre (vf.), to deduce,
    deduct
deludere (v.)*, to disappoint
deprimere (vf.), to depress
descrivere (vf.), to describe
detenere (vf.), to detain
detrarre (vf.), to detract,
    deduct
dieci (m.), ten
dietro behind
difendere (vf.), to defend
diffondere (v.), to diffuse,
    spread
dimetter(si) (vf.), to resign
diminuire (vsc.), to diminish
dimostrare (v.), to
    demonstrate, show
dipendere (vf.), to depend,
    hang from
dipingere (v.), to depict,
    paint
dire (vf.), to say, tell
  benedire to bless
  contraddire to contradict
  disdire to unsay, retract
  interdire to interdict,
      forbid
  maledire to curse
  predire to predict
  ridire to repeat, find
      fault with
dirigere (v.), to direct
discendere (vf.), to descend,
    come down from
discesa (f.), descent
discorrere (vf.), to
    discourse, chat
disdire (vf.), to unsay,
    retract
disfare (vf.), to unmake, undo
disgiungere (vf.), to unjoin

disporre (vf.), to dispose, arrange
dissentire (v.), to dissent
distendere (vf.), to distend
distruggere (v.), to destroy
divenire (vf.), to become
diventare (v.), to become
domanda (f.), question
domandare (v.), to ask
domani (m.), tomorrow
dopo after
dormire (v.), to sleep
dormita (f.), sleep
dovere (v.), to have to, must
drogheria (f.)*, general store
due (m.), two
dunque well then; therefore
educazione (f.)*, upbringing
eleggere (v.), to elect
eludere (v.), to elude
emettere (vf.), to emit
entrare (v.), to enter
entrata (f.), entrance
escludere (v.), to exclude
esporre (vf.), to expose
espresso express
esprimere (vf.), to express
essere (v.), to be
estendere (vf.), to extend
estrarre (vf.), to extract
evadere (v.), to evade
eventualmente* if, in case
evidente evident
evitare (v.), to avoid
fa ago
fabbrica (f.)*, factory
fare (v.), to do, make
  assuefare to accustom, get used to
  contraffare to counterfeit
  disfare to unmake, undo
  rifare to make again
  sfare to undo
  soddisfare to satisfy
  sopraffare to overwhelm
  torrefare to roast
  tumefare to tumefy, cause to swell
fare le spese go shopping
fatto (m.), fact
fattoria (f.)*, farm
fendere (vf.), to cut, fend off

difendere to defend
  fendere to cut, fend off
  offendere to offend
fermare (v.), to stop, halt
fiamma (f.), flame
fianco (m.), flank
fiducia (f.), trust, faith
figgere (v.), to fix (in place)
fingere (v.), to feign, pretend
finire (vsc.), to finish
fiore (m.), flower
fortunato lucky, fortunate
fra between, within, in
fraporre (vf.), to interpose
fratello (m.), brother
frequentare (v.), to frequent, attend
frequente frequent
frequenza (f.), frequency
friggere (v.), to fry
fungere (da) (v.), to function (as)
funzione (f.), function
fuori outside
genitori (m&f.), parents
gentilezza (f.), kindness
gettare (v.), to throw
getto (m.), throw
gettone (m.), token, phone slug
giorno (m.), day
girare (v.), to turn, spin
giro (m.), spin, outing
giungere (vf.), to arrive
  aggiungere to add
  congiungere to conjoin
  disgiungere to unjoin
  ingiungere to enjoin
  raggiungere to reach
  soggiungere to add verbally
  sopraggiungere to arrive unexpectedly
giù down
guadagnare (v.), to gain, earn
guardare (v.), to look at
ignorare (v.)*, to be ignorant of; pay no attention to
immettere (vf.), to let in
impiegato(a) (m&f.), employee
imporre (vf.), to impose
in in, into
incedere (vf.), to walk
incidente (m.)*, accident,

incident
includere (v.), to include
incontrare (v.), to encounter,
    meet
incontro (m.), encounter,
    meeting
indurre (vf.), to induce
infastidire (v.)*, to bother,
    be bothersome
infatti in fact
infondere (v.), to infuse
ingiungere (vf.), to enjoin
ingombrare (v.), to block,
    encumber
ininterrotto uninterrupted
iniziare (v.), to start
inizio (m.), start, beginning
insomma in sum; in conclusion
insorgere (v.), to rebel
intendere (vf.)*, to
    understand, intend
interdire (vf.), to interdict,
    forbid
interrotto interupted
intervenire (vf.), to intervene
intraprendere (vf.), to
    undertake
introdurre (vf.), to introduce
intromettere (vf.), to insert,
    intrude
invadere (v.), to invade
involgere (vf.)*, to wrap up
iscrivere (vf.), to inscribe,
    enroll
ispirare (v.), to inspire
istituto (m.), institute
lago (m.), lake
largo* wide
là there
legge (f.), law
leggere (v.), to read
libreria (f.)*, bookstore,
    bookshelf
litigio (m.), angry argument
lì there
macchina da scrivere (f.),
    typewriter
madre (f.), mother
magari if only
magazzino (m.)*, storage area
male bad, evil
maledire (vf.), to curse

malgoverno (m.), misgovernment
mantenere (vf.), to maintain
meraviglioso marvellous
mercato (m.), store
mese (m.), month
mettere (vf.), to place, put
  ammettere to admit
  commettere to commit
  compromettere to compromise
  dimetter(si) to resign
  emettere to emit
  immettere to let in
  intromettere to insert,
      intrude
  omettere to omit
  permettere to permit
  premettere to premise,
      place before
  promettere to promise
  rimettere to remit
  ripromotter(si) to propose
  scommettere to wager, bet
  smettere to stop, cease
  sottometter(si) to submit
  trasmettere to transmit
mica at all; perchance
mille (m.), one thousand
morbido* soft, delicate
morboso morbid, unhealthy
mordere (v.), to bite
morire (v.), to die
morte (f.), death
muovere (vf.), to move, stir
  commuovere* to move
      emotionally
  promuovere to promote
  rimuovere to move again,
      remove
nascondere (v.), to hide
necessità (f.), necessity
negozio (m.)*, store
nonna (f.), grandmother
nonno (m.), grandfather
notizie (f.), news
nove (m.), nine
obbedire (vsc.), to obey
occorrere (vf.)*, to be
    necessary
offendere (vf.), to offend
offesa (f.), offence
oggi (m.), today
omettere (vf.), to omit

opporre (vf.), to oppose
opportunità (f.), opportunity
opprimere (vf.), to oppress
ora now
ottendere (vf.), to obtend
ottenere (vf.), to obtain
otto (m.), eight
ovvio obvious
padre (m.), father
panorama (m.), panorama
paragonare (v.), to compare
parenti (m&f.)*, relatives
parlare (v.), to talk, speak
partenza (f.), departure
passare (v.), to pass
passato past
pendere (vf.), to hang
  appendere to append, hang up
  dipendere to depend, hang
    from
  propendere to be inclined
  sospendere to suspend
per through
perciò therefore
perdere (v.), to lose
permanente permanent
permesso (m.), permission
permettere (vf.), to permit
però however
persuadere (v.), to persuade
piacere (n) (m.), pleasure
piacere (vb) (v.), to be
    pleasing to
piangere (v.), to cry
piano (m.), floor, plan
piatto (m.), plate
piccolezza (f.), smallness
piccolo small
poco little
poi then
popolo (m.), people
porre (vf.), to put, place
  comporre to compose
  disporre to dispose, arrange
  esporre to expose
  imporre to impose
  opporre to oppose
  posporre to postpone
  proporre to propose
  riporre to put back, away
  scomporre to decompose
  sottoporre to submit

supporre to suppose
trasporre to transpose
posporre (vf.), to postpone
possibilità (f.),
    possibility, chance
potere (v.), to be able to, can
povero poor
pratica (f.), practice
praticare (v.), to practice
precedere (vf.), to precede
precisare (v.), to specify, be
    precise
prediligere (v.), to prefer,
    have a predilection for
predire (vf.), to predict
preferire (vsc.), to prefer
prefisso (m.), prefix, area
    code (phone)
premere (vf.), to press
  comprimere to compress
  deprimere to depress
  esprimere to express
  opprimere to oppress
  reprimere to repress
  sopprimere to suppress
  spremere to squeeze out
premettere (vf.), to premise,
    place before
prendere (vf.), to take, seize
  apprendere* to learn
  comprendere to comprise,
    include
  intraprendere to undertake
  riprendere to resume, take
    up again
  sorprendere to surprise
prescrivere (vf.), to prescribe
prestare (vf.), to lend
pretendere (vf.)*, to claim
prevedere (v.), to forecast
prevenire (vf.), to forewarn
prezzo (m.), price
prima before
primo first
problema (m.), problem
procedere (vf.), to proceed
produrre (vf.), to produce
promessa (f.), promise
promettere (vf.), to promise
promuovere (vf.), to promote
propendere (vf.), to be
    inclined

proporre (vf.), to propose
proprio really, one's own
proscrivere (vf.), to proscribe
prossimo next
proteggere (v.), to protect
protendere (vf.), to stretch
    out
protetto protected
protrarre (vf.), to protract,
    prolong
provenire (vf.), to come from
provvedere (v.), to provide
pubblicare (v.), to publish
pubblicazione (f.), publication
punto (m.), point, period
qua here
quarto fourth
quattro (m.), four
qui here
quindi therefore
quinto fifth
raccogliere (vf.), to pick up
    again
raggiungere (vf.), to reach
rapimento (m.)*, abduction
rapina (f.)*, robbery
rapinare (v.)*, to rob
rapire (v.)*, to kidnap, abduct
ratto (m.)*, rape, abduction;
    rat
realizzare (v.)*, to make
    something real
regalare (v.), to give a gift
regalo (m.), gift
registrare (v.)*, to record
    (as on tape)
regola (f.), regulation, rule
regolare (v.), to regulate,
    rule
rendere (v.), to render, give
    back
rendersi conto (v.), to
    realize (mentally)
reprimere (vf.), to repress
respingere (v.), to reject,
    push away
restare (vf.), to remain
riassumere (v.), to summarize
ricevere (v.), to receive
ricevuta (f.), receipt
riconoscere (v.), to recognize
ricordare (v.), to remember

ricordo (m.), remembrance,
    souvenir
ricorrere (vf.), to recur,
    have recourse to
ridere (v.), to smile, laugh
ridire (vf.), to repeat, find
    fault with
ridurre (vf.), to reduce
rifare (vf.), to make again
rimettere (vf.), to remit
rimuovere (vf.), to move
    again, remove
rincrescere (vf.), to regret
rinvenire (vf.), to come up
riporre (vf.), to put back,
    away
riprendere (vf.), to resume,
    take up again
riproduzione (f.), reproduction
riprometter(si) (vf.), to
    propose
riscrivere (vf.), to write
    again
riso (m.), rice
rispondere (v.), to respond,
    answer
risposta (f.), response, answer
ritenere (vf.), to retain
ritornare (v.), to return
ritorno (m.), return
ritrarre (vf.), to retract,
    deal with something again
riuscire (vsc.), to succeed
    at, manage
rivelare (v.), to reveal
rivista (f.), periodical,
    magazine
rivolgersi (vf.), to direct
    one's self towards, address
rompere (v.), to break, rupture
rotondo round, rotund
rottura (f.), break, rupture
rubare (v.), to steal
sale (m.), salt
salire (v.), to climb, ascend
salvare (v.), to save
sapere (v.), to know a thing,
    know how to do something
scambiare (v.), to exchange
scambio (m.), exchange
scappare (v.), to escape
scaricare (v.), to discharge,

scegliere (vf.), to select, choose

scelta (f.), choice, selection

scendere (vf.), to descend, come down from

  ascendere to ascend, climb

  discendere to descend, come down from

scherzare (v.), to joke, jest

scherzo (m.), joke, jest

sciogliere (vf.), to dissolve, untie

scommessa (f.), bet, wager

scommettere (vf.), to wager, bet

scomporre (vf.), to decompose

sconfiggere (v.), to defeat, overturn

scontare (v.), to discount

sconto (m.), discount

sconvolgere (vf.), to confuse seriously

scoperta (f.), discovery

scoprire (v.), to discover

scorso past

scrittura (f.), writing(s)

scrivere (vf.), to write

  ascrivere to ascribe

  descrivere to describe

  iscrivere to inscribe, enroll

  prescrivere to prescribe

  proscrivere to proscribe

  riscrivere to write again

  sottoscrivere to subscribe, underwrite

  trascrivere to transcribe

scusare (v.), to excuse

secondo ... according to ...

sedersi (v.), to seat one's self

sedurre (vf.), to seduce

seduta (f.), session, seating

sei (m.), six

sentire (v.), to hear, feel, sense

servizio (m.), service

sette (m.), seven

settimana (f.), week

sfare (vf.), to undo

sfiducia (f.), mistrust

sfortunato unfortunate, unlucky

sicuro sure, secure

signora (f.), madam, Mrs.

signore (m.), sir, Mr.

signorina (f.), nubile woman, Miss

sistema (m.), system

sistemar(si) (v.), to put in order; (si) settle one's self in

smettere (vf.), to stop, cease

soccorrere (vf.), to succor, help

soddisfare (vf.), to satisfy

soddisfatto satisfied

soggiungere (vf.), to add verbally

sopprimere (vf.), to suppress

sopra above

sopraffare (vf.), to overwhelm

sopraggiungere (vf.), to arrive unexpectedly

sopravvenire (vf.), to supervene, turn up

sorella (f.), sister

sorgere (v.), to rise

sorprendere (vf.), to surprise

sorpreso surprised

sospendere (vf.), to suspend

sostanza (f.), substance

sostare (vf.), to stop, pause

sostenere (vf.), to support, hold up

sotto under

sottolineare (v.), to emphasize

sottometter(si) (vf.), to submit

sottoporre (vf.), to submit

sottoscrivere (vf.), to subscribe, underwrite

sottostare (vf.), to be below

sottrarre (vf.), to subtract, steal

sovrastare (vf.), to dominate

sovrintendere (vf.), to superintend

sovvenire (vf.), to remember

spendere (v.), to spend

spese (f.), expenses

  fare le spese go shopping

spiegare (v.), to explain

spiegazione (f.), explanation

spingere (v.), to push
spinta (f.), push, shove
spremere (vf.), to squeeze out
stare (v.), to be, stand
  constatare to ascertain
  contrastare to contrast
  costare to cost
  prestare to lend
  restare to remain
  sostare to stop, pause
  sottostare to be below
  sovrastare to dominate
stendere (vf.), to hang, extend
storia (f.)*, history
strada (f.), street, road
stravolgere (vf.), to confuse
    meanings
stringere (v.), to squeeze,
    tighten
studiare (v.), to study
studio (m.), study
su up
succedere (vf.)*, to happen
supporre (vf.), to suppose
svenire (vf.), to faint
sviluppare (v.), to develop
sviluppo (m.), development
svolgere (vf.), to carry out,
    take to a point
svolgersi (vf.), to take place
tagliare (v.), to cut
tavola (f.), table
tema (m.), theme
tendere (vf.), to stretch,
    tighten
  attendere* to await, expect
  contendere to contend
  distendere to distend
  estendere to extend
  intendere* to understand,
    intend
  ottendere to obtend
  pretendere* to claim
  protendere to stretch out
  sovrintendere to superintend
  stendere to hang, extend
tenere (vf.), to keep, hold
  appartenere* to belong (to)
  attener(si)* to stick with
  contenere to contain
  detenere to detain

  mantenere to maintain
  ottenere to obtain
  ritenere to retain
  sostenere to support, hold
    up
  trattenere to hold back,
    detain
tentare (v.), to attempt
tesi (f.), thesis
tingere (v.), to tint, dye
tinta (f.), ink, tint, dye
toccare (v.), to touch
tocco (m.), touch
togliere (vf.), to take away
  accogliere to greet, welcome
  cogliere to collect
  raccogliere to pick up again
  scegliere to select, choose
  sciogliere to dissolve,
    untie
torrefare (vf.), to roast
tradire (v.), to betray
tradurre (vf.)*, to translate
transazione (f.), transaction
transizione (f.), transition
trarre (vf.), to draw, pull
  astrarre to abstract
  contrarre to contract
  detrarre to detract, deduct
  estrarre to extract
  protrarre to protract,
    prolong
  ritrarre to retract, deal
    with something again
  sottrarre to subtract, steal
trascorrere (vf.), to pass time
trascrivere (vf.), to
    transcribe
trasmettere (vf.), to transmit
trasporre (vf.), to transpose
trattamento (m.), treatment
trattare (v.), to treat
trattenere (vf.), to hold
    back, detain
travolgere (vf.), to upset,
    throw into confusion
tre (m.), three
trenta (m.), thirty
tumefare (vf.), to tumefy,
    cause to swell
uccidere (v.), to kill
università (f.), university

uno (m.), one
uscire (vsc.), to exit, go out
utile useful, utilizable
valutare (v.), to evaluate
vedere (v.), to see, view
venire (v.), to come
  avvenire to happen, occur
  contravvenire to contravene
  convenire to convene
  divenire to become
  intervenire to intervene
  prevenire to forewarn
  provenire to come from
  rinvenire to come up
  sopravvenire to supervene,
     turn up
  sovvenire to remember
  svenire to faint
venti (m.), twenty
verità (f.), truth
vestire (v.), to dress, clothe
vestito (m.), clothes, suit
viaggio (m.), voyage, trip
vicino (a) near
violentare (v.)*, to rape
violenza carnale (f.), rape

vista (f.), view
volare (v.), to fly
volere (v.), to want, wish
volgare vulgar
volgere (vf.), to turn
  avvolgere to wrap around
  capovolgere to turn upside
     down
  coinvolgere to involve
     together
  involgere* to wrap up
  rivolgersi to direct one's
     self towards, address
  sconvolgere to confuse
     seriously
  stravolgere to confuse
     meanings
  svolgere to carry out, take
     to a point
  svolgersi to take place
  travolgere to upset, throw
     into confusion
volo (m.), flight
volta (f.), time, turn
zia (f.), aunt
zio (m.), uncle

Italian nouns, verbs, and Unfaithful Cognates are identified as such in this listing. The abbreviations used are as follows:

(f.) = feminine noun

(m.) = masculine noun

(m&f.) = masculine and/or feminine noun

* = Unfaithful Cognate

(v.) = plain verb, neither member of a family nor an **-isco** verb

(vf.) = verb which is a member of a family

(vsc.) = verb of **-isco** type

Verbs which are members of families, carrying the "(vf.)" designation, are listed under the main verb with all other family members in the Italian-English Vocabulary. Likewise, descriptions of families are listed in the Index. For instance, **astrarre** is listed under **trarre** in both the Italian-English Vocabulary and in the Index.

abduction rapimento (m.)*
above sopra
to **abstract** astrarre (vf.)
accident, incident incidente (m.)*
accident, mishap accidente (m.)
according to ... secondo ...
to **accustom, get used to** assuefar(si) (vf.)
act atto (m.)
to **add** aggiungere (vf.)
to **add verbally** soggiungere (vf.)
to **adduce** addurre (vf.)
adjective aggettivo (m.)
to **admit** ammettere (vf.)
affix affisso (m.)
affront affronto (m.)
after dopo
ago fa
ahead, forward avanti
angry argument litigio (m.)

aperture, opening apertura (f.)
to **append, hang up** appendere (vf.)
to **approach, comply with** accedere (vf.)
arrival arrivo (m.)
to **arrive** arrivare (v.)
to **arrive unexpectedly** sopraggiungere (vf.)
artist artista (m&f.)
as, from da
to **ascend, climb** ascendere (vf.)
to **ascertain** constatare (vf.)
to **ascribe** ascrivere (vf.)
to **ask** domandare (v.)
at all; perchance mica
to **attempt** tentare (v.)
to **attract, draw** attrarre (vf.)
aunt zia (f.)
to **avoid** evitare (v.)

to **await, expect** attendere
    (vf.)*
baby, child bambino(a) (m&f.)
bad, evil male
to **be** essere (v.)
to **be able to, can** potere (v.)
to **be below** sottostare (vf.)
to **be bored** annoiar(si) (v.)*
to **be ignorant of; pay no**
    attention to ignorare
    (v.)*
to **be inclined** propendere
    (vf.)
to **be necessary** occorrere
    (vf.)*
to **be pleasing to** piacere
    (vb) (v.)
to **be, stand** stare (v.)
to **be, stay** stare (vf.)
to **beat** battere (v.)
to **become** diventare (v.)
before prima
behind dietro
to **believe** credere (v.)
to **belong (to)** appartenere
    (vf.)*
benediction benedizione (f.)
benevolence benevolenza (f.)
bet, wager scommessa (f.)
to **betray** tradire (v.)
between, within, in fra
to **bite** mordere (v.)
to **bless** benedire (vf.)
to **block, encumber** ingombrare
    (v.)
bookstore, bookshelf libreria
    (f.)*
to **bother, be bothersome**
    infastidire (v.)*
brave, courageous coraggioso
break, rupture rottura (f.)
brief, short breve
brother fratello (m.)
to **burn** ardere (v.)
to **buy** comprare (v.)
to **call** chiamare (v.)
call, phone call chiamata (f.)
to **carry out, take to a point**
    svolgere (vf.)
to **cede, yield** cedere (vf.)
to **change, exchange money**
    cambiare (v.)

change, money exchange cambio
    (m.)
to **charge, load** caricare (v.)
to **chat, gossip** chiacchierare
    (v.)
choice, selection scelta (f.)
to **cinch, gird** cingere (v.)
city città (f.)
to **claim** pretendere (vf.)*
clear chiaro
clerk commesso(a) (m&f.)
clever, good bravo
climate clima (m.)
to **climb, ascend** salire (v.)
to **close** chiudere (v.)
clothes, suit vestito (m.)
to **coincide** coincidere (v.)
to **collect** cogliere (vf.)
to **come** venire (v.)
to **come from** provenire (vf.)
to **come up** rinvenire (vf.)
to **commence, begin** cominciare
    (v.)
to **commit** commettere (vf.)
communist comunista (m&f.)
to **compare** paragonare (v.)
to **compete, concur** concorrere
    (vf.)
to **compose** comporre (vf.)
to **compress** comprimere (vf.)
to **comprise, include**
    comprendere (vf.)
to **compromise** compromettere
    (vf.)
to **concede** concedere (vf.)
to **conclude** concludere (v.)
conclusion conclusione (f.)
to **conduct** condurre (vf.)
conflict conflitto (m.)
to **confound, confuse**
    confondere (v.)
to **confuse meanings**
    stravolgere (vf.)
to **confuse seriously**
    sconvolgere (vf.)
to **conjoin** congiungere (vf.)
conspicuous cospicuo
to **conspire** cospirare (v.)
constant costante
to **constrain** costringere (v.)
to **construct, build** costruire
    (vsc.)

to **contain** contenere (vf.)
to **contend** contendere (vf.)
contentedness contentezza (f.)
to **continue** continuare (v.)
to **contract** contrarre (vf.)
to **contradict** contraddire (vf.)
to **contrast** contrastare (vf.)
to **contravene** contravvenire (vf.)
to **convene** convenire (vf.)
to **cook** cucinare (v.)
to **correct** correggere (v.)
to **cost** costare (vf.)
to **counterfeit** contraffare (vf.)
cousin cugino(a) (m&f.)
crisis crisi (f.)
to **cry** piangere (v.)
currently, now attuale
to **curse** maledire (vf.)
to **cut** tagliare (v.)
to **cut, fend off** fendere (vf.)
dammit accidenti
day giorno (m.)
death morte (f.)
to **decompose** scomporre (vf.)
to **decrease** decrescere (vf.)
to **deduce, deduct** dedurre (vf.)
to **defeat, overturn** sconfiggere (v.)
to **defend** difendere (vf.)
to **demonstrate, show** dimostrare (v.)
departure partenza (f.)
to **depend, hang from** dipendere (vf.)
to **depict, paint** dipingere (v.)
to **depress** deprimere (vf.)
to **descend, come down from** discendere (vf.)
descent discesa (f.)
to **describe** descrivere (vf.)
to **destroy** distruggere (v.)
to **detain** detenere (vf.)
to **detract, deduct** detrarre (vf.)
to **develop** sviluppare (v.)
development sviluppo (m.)
to **die** decedere (vf.)

to **diffuse, spread** diffondere (v.)
to **diminish** diminuire (vsc.)
to **direct** dirigere (v.)
to **direct one's self towards, address** rivolgersi (vf.)
to **disappoint** deludere (v.)*
to **discharge, unload** scaricare (v.)
discount sconto (m.)
to **discourse, chat** discorrere (vf.)
to **discover** scoprire (v.)
discovery scoperta (f.)
to **dispose, arrange** disporre (vf.)
to **dissent** dissentire (v.)
to **dissolve, untie** sciogliere (vf.)
to **distend** distendere (vf.)
to **do, make** fare (v.)
to **dominate** sovrastare (vf.)
down giù
to **draw, pull** trarre (vf.)
to **dress, clothe** vestire (v.)
to **drink** bere (v.)
drink, beverage bibita (f.)
eight otto (m.)
to **elect** eleggere (v.)
to **elude** eludere (v.)
embrace abbraccio (m.)
to **emit** emettere (vf.)
to **emphasize** sottolineare (v.)
employee impiegato(a) (m&f.)
to **enclose, include** accludere (v.)
to **encounter, meet** incontrare (v.)
encounter, meeting incontro (m.)
to **enjoin** ingiungere (vf.)
to **enter** entrare (v.)
entrance entrata (f.)
to **escape** scappare (v.)
to **evade** evadere (v.)
to **evaluate** valutare (v.)
evident evidente
exchange scambio (m.)
to **exclude** escludere (v.)
to **excuse** scusare (v.)
to **exit, go out** uscire (vsc.)
expenses spese (f.)

to **explain** spiegare (v.)
explanation spiegazione (f.)
to **expose** esporre (vf.)
to **express** esprimere (vf.)
to **extend** estendere (vf.)
to **extract** estrarre (vf.)
to **face, confront** affrontare (v.)*
fact fatto (m.)
factory fabbrica (f.)*
to **faint** svenire (vf.)
farm fattoria (f.)*
father padre (m.)
to **feign, pretend** fingere (v.)
fifth quinto
fifty cinquanta (m.)
to **finish** finire (vsc.)
first primo
five cinque (m.)
to **fix (in place)** figgere (v.)
flame fiamma (f.)
flank fianco (m.)
flight volo (m.)
floor, plan piano (m.)
flower fiore (m.)
to **fly** volare (v.)
to **forecast** prevedere (v.)
to **forewarn** prevenire (vf.)
four quattro (m.)
fourth quarto
frequency frequenza (f.)
frequent frequente
to **frequent, attend** frequentare (v.)
to **fry** friggere (v.)
function funzione (f.)
to **function (as)** fungere (da) (v.)
to **gain, earn** guadagnare (v.)
general store drogheria (f.)*
to **get up, rise up** alzarsi (v.)
getting up, rising up alzata (f.)
gift regalo (m.)
to **give a gift** regalare (v.)
to **give, confer** dare (v.)
to **go** andare (v.)
go shopping fare le spese
grandfather nonno (m.)
grandmother nonna (f.)
to **greet, welcome** accogliere (vf.)

growth crescita (f.)
to **hang** pendere (vf.)
to **hang, extend** stendere (vf.)
to **happen** capitare (v.)
to **happen, occur** avvenire (vf.)
to **have** avere (v.)
to **have to, must** dovere (v.)
to **hear, feel, sense** sentire (v.)
height altezza (f.)
help, aid aiuto (m.)
here qui
to **hide** nascondere (v.)
hill collina (f.)
history storia (f.)*
to **hold back, detain** trattenere (vf.)
however comunque
if only magari
if, in case eventualmente
to **impose** imporre (vf.)
in fact infatti
in front of davanti (a)
in sum; in conclusion insomma
in, into in
to **include** includere (v.)
to **increase** accrescere (vf.)
to **increase, grow** crescere (vf.)
to **induce** indurre (vf.)
to **infuse** infondere (v.)
ink, tint, dye tinta (f.)
to **inscribe, enroll** iscrivere (vf.)
to **insert, intrude** intromettere (vf.)
to **inspect, control** controllare (v.)*
inspection controllo (m.)*
to **inspire** ispirare (v.)
institute istituto (m.)
to **interdict, forbid** interdire (vf.)
to **interpose** fraporre (vf.)
interupted interrotto
to **intervene** intervenire (vf.)
to **introduce** introdurre (vf.)
to **invade** invadere (v.)
to **involve together** coinvolgere (vf.)
joke, jest scherzo (m.)

to **keep, hold** tenere (vf.)
to **kidnap, abduct** rapire (v.)*
to **kill** uccidere (v.)
kindness gentilezza (f.)
kitchen cucina (f.)
to **know a person or place** conoscere (v.)
to **know a thing, know how to do something** sapere (v.)
lake lago (m.)
law legge (f.)
lawyer, advocate avvocato (m.)
to **learn** apprendere (vf.)*
to **lend** prestare (vf.)
to **let in** immettere (vf.)
library biblioteca (f.)
to **light, kindle** accendere (v.)
little poco
to **look at** guardare (v.)
to **lose** perdere (v.)
love amore (m.)
lucky, fortunate fortunato
madam, Mrs. signora (f.)
to **maintain** mantenere (vf.)
to **make again** rifare (vf.)
to **make one's self comfortable** accomodarsi (v.)
to **make something real** realizzare (v.)*
to **make, do** fare (vf.)
marvellous meraviglioso
misgovernment malgoverno (m.)
mistrust sfiducia (f.)
moment attimo (m.)
month mese (m.)
morbid, unhealthy morboso
mother madre (f.)
to **move again, remove** rimuovere (vf.)
to **move emotionally** commuovere (vf.)*
to **move, stir** muovere (vf.)
near vicino (a)
necessity necessità (f.)
news notizie (f.)
next prossimo
nine nove (m.)
to **notice** accorgersi (v.)
notice, warning avviso (m.)*
now adesso
nubile woman, Miss signorina (f.)

to **obey** obbedire (vsc.)
to **obtain** ottenere (vf.)
to **obtend** ottendere (vf.)
obvious ovvio
offence offesa (f.)
to **offend** offendere (vf.)
to **omit** omettere (vf.)
one uno (m.)
one hundred cento (m.)
one thousand mille (m.)
to **open** aprire (v.)
opportunity opportunità (f.)
to **oppose** opporre (vf.)
to **oppress** opprimere (vf.)
outside fuori
to **overwhelm** sopraffare (vf.)
panorama panorama (m.)
parents genitori (m&f.)
to **pass** passare (v.)
to **pass time** trascorrere (vf.)
past scorso
people popolo (m.)
periodical, magazine rivista (f.)
permanent permanente
permission permesso (m.)
to **permit** permettere (vf.)
to **persuade** persuadere (v.)
to **pick up again** raccogliere (vf.)
to **place, put** mettere (vf.)
plate piatto (m.)
pleasure piacere (m.)
point, period punto (m.)
poor povero
possibility, chance possibilità (f.)
to **postpone** posporre (vf.)
to **practice** praticare (v.)
to **precede** antecedere (vf.)
to **predict** predire (vf.)
to **prefer** preferire (vsc.)
to **prefer, have a predilection for** prediligere (v.)
prefix, area code (phone) prefisso (m.)
to **premise, place before** premettere (vf.)
to **prescribe** prescrivere (vf.)
to **press** premere (vf.)
price prezzo (m.)
problem problema (m.)

to **proceed** procedere (vf.)
to **produce** produrre (vf.)
to **promise** promettere (vf.)
to **promote** promuovere (vf.)
to **propose** riprometter(si) (vf.)
to **proscribe** proscrivere (vf.)
to **protect** proteggere (v.)
protected protetto
to **protract, prolong** protrarre (vf.)
to **provide** provvedere (v.)
publication pubblicazione (f.)
to **publish** pubblicare (v.)
to **push** spingere (v.)
push, shove spinta (f.)
to **put back, away** riporre (vf.)
to **put in order; (si) settle one's self in** sistemar(si) (v.)
to **put, place** porre (vf.)
question domanda (f.)
rape violenza carnale (f.)
rape, abduction; rat ratto (m.)*
to **reach** raggiungere (vf.)
to **read** leggere (v.)
to **realize (mentally)** rendersi conto (v.)
really, one's own proprio
to **rebel** insorgere (v.)
receipt ricevuta (f.)
to **receive** ricevere (v.)
to **recognize** riconoscere (v.)
to **record (as on tape)** registrare (v.)*
to **recur, have recourse to** ricorrere (vf.)
to **reduce** ridurre (vf.)
to **regret** rincrescere (vf.)
to **regulate, rule** regolare (v.)
regulation, rule regola (f.)
to **reject, push away** respingere (v.)
relatives parenti (m&f.)*
to **remain** restare (vf.)
to **remember** ricordare (v.)
remembrance, souvenir ricordo (m.)
to **remit** rimettere (vf.)

to **render, give back** rendere (v.)
to **repeat, find fault with** ridire (vf.)
to **repress** reprimere (vf.)
reproduction riproduzione (f.)
to **resign** dimetter(si) (vf.)
to **respond, answer** rispondere (v.)
response, answer risposta (f.)
to **resume, take up again** riprendere (vf.)
to **retain** ritenere (vf.)
to **retract, deal with something again** ritrarre (vf.)
return ritorno (m.)
to **reveal** rivelare (v.)
rice riso (m.)
to **rise** sorgere (v.)
to **roast** torrefare (vf.)
to **rob** rapinare (v.)*
robbery rapina (f.)*
room camera (f.)*
round, rotund rotondo
to **run** correre (vf.)
to **run, rush** accorrere (vf.)
salt sale (m.)
satisfied soddisfatto
to **satisfy** soddisfare (vf.)
to **save** salvare (v.)
to **say, tell** dire (vf.)
to **seat one's self** sedersi (v.)
to **seduce** sedurre (vf.)
to **see, view** vedere (v.)
to **seek, search for** cercare (v.)
to **select, choose** scegliere (vf.)
service servizio (m.)
session, seating seduta (f.)
seven sette (m.)
sir, Mr. signore (m.)
sister sorella (f.)
six sei (m.)
sleep dormita (f.)
small piccolo
smallness piccolezza (f.)
to **smile, laugh** ridere (v.)
soft, delicate morbido
to **specify, be precise** precisare (v.)

to **spend** spendere (v.)
spin, outing giro (m.)
to **sprinkle** aspergere (v.)*
to **squeeze out** spremere (vf.)
to **squeeze, tighten** stringere
   (v.)
to **start** iniziare (v.)
start, beginning inizio (m.)
steak, beefsteak bistecca (f.)
to **steal** rubare (v.)
to **stick with** attener(si)
   (vf.)*
still, yet ancora
to **stop, cease** smettere (vf.)
to **stop, halt** fermare (v.)
to **stop, pause** sostare (vf.)
storage area magazzino (m.)*
store negozio (m.)*
street, road strada (f.)
to **stretch out** protendere
   (vf.)
to **stretch, tighten** tendere
   (vf.)
study studio (m.)
to **submit** sottoporre (vf.)
to **subscribe, underwrite**
   sottoscrivere (vf.)
substance sostanza (f.)
to **subtract, steal** sottrarre
   (vf.)
to **succeed at, manage**
   riuscire (vsc.)
to **succor, help** soccorrere
   (vf.)
to **summarize** riassumere (v.)
to **superintend** sovrintendere
   (vf.)
to **supervene, turn up**
   sopravvenire (vf.)
to **support, hold up** sostenere
   (vf.)
to **suppose** supporre (vf.)
to **suppress** sopprimere (vf.)
sure, secure sicuro
to **surprise** sorprendere (vf.)
surprised sorpreso
to **suspend** sospendere (vf.)
system sistema (m.)
table tavola (f.)
to **take away** togliere (vf.)
to **take place** svolgersi (vf.)
to **take, seize** prendere (vf.)

to **talk, speak** parlare (v.)
ten dieci (m.)
that is cioè
theme tema (m.)
then allora
then, after that poi
then, at that time allora
there lì
there, ourselves ci
therefore quindi
thesis tesi (f.)
thirty trenta (m.)
three tre (m.)
through per
throw getto (m.)
time, turn volta (f.)
to **tint, dye** tingere (v.)
to, at, in a
today oggi (m.)
token, phone slug gettone (m.)
tomorrow domani (m.)
topic of discourse argomento
   (m.)*
touch tocco (m.)
transaction transazione (f.)
to **transcribe** trascrivere
   (vf.)
transition transizione (f.)
to **translate** tradurre (vf.)*
to **transmit** trasmettere (vf.)
to **transpose** trasporre (vf.)
to **treat** trattare (v.)
treatment trattamento (m.)
trust, faith fiducia (f.)
truth verità (f.)
to **tumefy, cause to swell**
   tumefare (vf.)
to **turn** volgere (vf.)
to **turn upside down**
   capovolgere (vf.)
to **turn, spin** girare (v.)
twenty venti (m.)
two due (m.)
typewriter macchina da
   scrivere (f.)
uncle zio (m.)
under sotto
to **understand** capire (vsc.)
to **understand, intend**
   intendere (vf.)*
to **undertake** intraprendere
   (vf.)

to **undo** sfare (vf.)
unfortunate, unlucky
    sfortunato
uninterrupted ininterrotto
university università (f.)
to **unjoin** disgiungere (vf.)
to **unmake, undo** disfare (vf.)
to **unsay, retract** disdire (vf.)
up su
upbringing educazione (f.)*
to **upset, throw into confusion**
    travolgere (vf.)
useful, utilizable utile
view vista (f.)
voyage, trip viaggio (m.)
vulgar volgare
to **wager, bet** scommettere (vf.)

to **wait** aspettare (v.)
waiting attesa (f.)
to **walk** camminare (v.)
to **want, wish** volere (v.)
weak debole
week settimana (f.)
well then; therefore dunque
well, good bene
wide largo*
to **wrap around** avvolgere (vf.)
to **wrap up** involgere (vf.)*
to **write** scrivere (vf.)
to **write again** riscrivere (vf.)
writing(s) scrittura (f.)
year anno (m.)
yield, cede cedere (vf.)
zoo giardino zoologico (m.)

a (Firenze) in (a city, e.g. Florence)
a due passi a few steps
a metà (mezza) strada halfway
a piedi on foot
a posto ok; in good order
acqua in bocca! don't breathe a word of it!
ad ogni modo in any case
al dente cooked firm
al di là beyond, past
alle (dieci) at (ten o'clock)
altro che! of course; you betcha!
andare bene, male to go well, poorly
avercela to have had it with someone, something
avere (67) anni to be (67) years old
basta così that's enough
bo!; boh! so what!; well!; so!
ci vuole, vogliono it takes
cin cin cheers (drinking toast)
come al solito as usual
come mai?! how come?!; how could this ever be?!
da (Mario) to (a person's house, e.g. Mario's)
da (time) in poi (present perfect) since, from the time when (followed by present perfect)
da ora in poi from now on, henceforth
da quando (present tense) since, from the time when (followed by present tense)
da una volta all'altra from one time to the next
dal(le nove) al(le undici) from (nine o'clock) to (eleven o'clock)
dare fastidio to bother, cause discomfort
davanti a in front of
di giorno in giorno day by day (progressive)
di tanto in tanto from time to time
di volta in volta from one time to the next
dimmi! tell me! (informal)
eh, già ah, yes
essere pieno di sè to be full of one's self
faccia pure! do as you wish, please! (formal)
fammelo vedere! show it to me! (informal)
fare un brindisi to make a toast
fare una bella figura to cut a fine figure, make a good impression
figurati! don't mention it!
fin da ever since, from
fino ad oggi; finora hitherto, until now
forza! let's get going!; onward!
fra (le nove) e (le undici) from (nine o'clock) to (eleven o'clock)
fra poco soon, in a little while
fregarsene to not give a damn
giorno per giorno day by day (non-progressive)
grosso modo by and large
in aereo(plano) by air(plane)
in anticipo early
in autobus by bus
in bicicletta by bicycle
in bocca al lupo! good luck!
in fondo at the back
in genere in general
in macchina by car
in orario on time (vehicle)
in ritardo late
in treno by train
intorno a around, near
l'ultima volta last time (of a series)
le ore sono (le tre) the time is (three o'clock)
lo spiritoso smart aleck

meno male just as well
mi dica! tell me! (formal)
mica male not bad (grudging
    approval)
neanche per sogno! not on
    your life!
non c'è male not bad
non fa niente it's nothing;
    not important
non fare complimenti don't be
    shy (out of courtesy)
ogni tanto from time to time
pasticcio; che pasticcio
    mess; what a mess
per quanto riguarda
    regarding; in regard to
piccolo paese little town;
    place in the countryside
punto e basta! that's it,
    period!
può darsi (subj) maybe (then
    subjunctive)
quarto d'ora quarter hour
quindici giorni fortnight,
    two weeks

rendersi conto to realize
    mentally
riuscire a to manage to,
    to succeed at
sbrigati! hurry up!
secondo (Einstein) ...
    according to Einstein ...
sede del governo seat of
    government, capital
sempre diritto straight ahead
senso unico one-way street
senz'altro but of course;
    without a doubt
senza dubbio without a doubt
si accomodi seat yourself;
    make yourself comfortable
    (formal)
smettila! stop it! (informal)
stanco morto dead tired
su e giù up and down
toccare a to be one's turn
vale la pena to be worth it;
    to be worth the trouble
vicino a close to, near

a few steps a due passi
according to (Einstein) ...
    secondo (Einstein) ...
ah, yes eh, già
around, near intorno a
as usual come al solito
at (ten o'clock) alle (dieci)
at the back in fondo
beyond, past al di là
but of course; without a doubt
    senz'altro
by air(plane) in aereo(plano)
by and large grosso modo
by bicycle in bicicletta
by bus in autobus
by car in macchina
by train in treno
cheers (drinking toast) cin
    cin
close to, near vicino a
cooked firm al dente
day by day (non-progressive)
    giorno per giorno
day by day (progressive) di
    giorno in giorno
dead tired stanco morto
do as you wish, please!
    (formal) faccia pure!
don't be shy (out of courtesy)
    non fare complimenti
don't breathe a word of it!
    acqua in bocca!
don't mention it! figurati!
early in anticipo
ever since, from fin da
fortnight, two weeks quindici
    giorni
from (nine o'clock) to (eleven
    o'clock) fra (le nove) e
    (le undici)
from now on, henceforth da
    ora in poi
from one time to the next di
    volta in volta
from time to time ogni tanto

good luck! in bocca al lupo!
halfway a metà (mezza) strada
hitherto, until now fino ad
    oggi; finora
how come?!; how could this ever
    be?! come mai?!
hurry up! sbrigati!
in (a city, e.g. Florence) a
    (Firenze)
in any case ad ogni modo
in front of davanti a
in general in genere
it takes ci vuole, vogliono
it's nothing; not important
    non fa niente
just as well meno male
last time (of a series)
    l'ultima volta
late in ritardo
let's get going!; onward!
    forza!
little town; place in the
    countryside piccolo paese
maybe (then subjunctive) può
    darsi (subj)
mess; what a mess pasticcio;
    che pasticcio
not bad non c'è male
not bad (grudging approval)
    mica male
not on your life! neanche per
    sogno!
of course; you betcha! altro
    che!
ok; in good order a posto
on foot a piedi
on time (vehicle) in orario
one-way (street) senso unico
quarter of an hour quarto
    d'ora
regarding, in regard to;
    concerning per quanto
    riguarda
seat of government, capital
    sede del governo

seat yourself; make yourself
    comfortable (formal) si
    accomodi
show it to me! (informal)
    fammelo vedere!
since, from the time when
    (followed by present
    perfect) da (time) in poi
    (+ present perfect)
smart aleck lo spiritoso
so what!; well!; who knows? boh!
soon, in a little while fra poco
stop it! (informal) smettila!
straight ahead sempre diritto
tell me! (formal) mi dica!
tell me! (informal) dimmi!
that's enough basta così
that's it, period! punto e
    basta!
the time is (eight a.m.)
    le ore sono (le otto)
    ... (one p.m.) (le tredici)

to (a person's house, e.g.
    Mario's) da (Mario)
to be (67) years old avere
    (67) anni
to be full of one's self
    essere pieno di sè
to be one's turn toccare a
to be worth it; to be worth the
    trouble vale la pena
to bother, cause discomfort
    dare fastidio
to cut a fine figure, make a
    good impression fare una
    bella figura
to go well, poorly andare
    bene, male
to manage to, to succeed at
    riuscire a
to realize (mentally)
    rendersi conto
up and down su e giù
without a doubt senza dubbio